DUTCH SOCIETY

STUDIES IN MODERN SOCIETIES

CONSULTING EDITOR:
CHARLES H. PAGE
University of California
Santa Cruz

A Random House Study in Sociology

DUTCH SOCIETY

Johan Goudsblom

UNIVERSITY OF AMSTERDAM

RANDOM HOUSE   New York

FIRST PRINTING

Manufactured in the United States of America by
H. Wolff Book Manufacturing Co., New York

Typography by Leon Bolognese

Editor's Introduction

Studies in Sociology, the first paperback series in the field, was planned primarily—though not exclusively—for use in undergraduate programs, in combination at the introductory level or as core readings in more specialized courses. This feature of the studies has persisted. However, in keeping with the spectacular growth of sociology, the series has not only grown vigorously, but its format has become more flexible. It now accommodates some "popular" or relatively lighthearted essays, some studies of subjects that might have been viewed in former years as sociologically marginal, and, especially, some more specialized contributions. The series on the social and cultural systems of national societies launched with this book is an example of this flexible expansion.

Dutch Society brings out the principal desiderata for these studies: First, no strict guidelines govern the organ-

ization of content or, indeed, the definition of what constitute the "major" components of the sociocultural system of
a national society. Such permissiveness carries risks, to be
sure, and is starkly inconsistent with abstract theoretical
formulations of "*the* structure of society" or of "*basic* institutions" or of "system requisites." But to adopt one or
the other of these categorical schemes would require the
selection of a single theoretical orientation for the series
and preclude diversity of approach, would prejudge theoretical issues still under hot dispute ("are industrial societies all alike?" continues to receive ambiguous answers),
and would therefore narrow authorship to scholars of a
single theoretical persuasion. Flexibility of approach and
format, then, is an important criterion of the series.

A second and contrasting criterion, however, is also il-
lustrated by *Dutch Society.* Dr. Goudsblom shares the
view of other contributors to this series (studies are well
under way on Brazil, Britain, France, Germany, Italy,
Poland, and Spain, with several more on the horizon)
that certain features of present-day national societies are
especially appropriate subjects for sociological treatment.
These include the principal social divisions, the directly
related strategic forces conducive to national integration
and strain, familial and communal patterns, developments
in "mass" or popular culture, and, with respect to all of
these, the sources and nature of social and cultural trends.
These emphases characterize the sociological perspective—
in contrast with the perspective of, say, economics and
political science—which marks *Dutch Society* and the
forthcoming studies in the series.

Another essential requirement of these studies is sound
scholarship, a requirement magnified by the necessity of
treating complex and often controversial subjects suc-
cinctly. There is very limited opportunity in these mod-
estly sized books for the speculative essay or theoretical

disputation. Yet the volumes in this series are not "hand-books" or elementary guides for casual browsing; rather, their aim is to provide a solid basis for serious *sociological* study of national societies. This goal, I believe, is accomplished by Dr. Goudsblom, who successfully manages to combine hard fact and suggestive interpretation.

The interdependent subjects of *continuity* and *change* constitute the chief focus of *Dutch Society*. These are not, as Dr. Goudsblom puts it at one point, "simple themes." But the persistences and transformations of institutional and cultural patterns are fundamental sociological concerns, and are, or should be, central themes in the comparative analysis of modern societies. Comparative study, stimulated by the growth of general theory and of international scholarly exchange, is rapidly becoming an important characteristic of the teaching enterprise of sociology, reflected in curricular innovations and in the content and orientation of textbooks such as this one. *Dutch Society,* and volumes like it, are primary sources for comparative sociological study.

Dutch Society is particularly appropriate as the initial study of this series, because although The Netherlands is a small country, within its limited area and population have emerged most of the dominant structural and cultural features of advanced "modernization": large-scale urbanization and suburbanization, industrial and technological sophistication, a rapidly changing class structure marked by considerable social mobility, multi-associations and a system of "countervailing power," widespread education and mass media, nucleation of the family and decline of the functional significance of the small community. These are familiar phenomena to American readers; *Dutch Society* shows how and why they have come about in a smaller nation with a far different economic, political, and cultural legacy. This points up another important educational use of Dr. Goudsblom's book: *Dutch Society* is a revealing case study in modernization.

Finally, the book is an excellent introduction to The Netherlands as such—for the student of the social sciences, to be sure, but also for the ubiquitous "general reader." When more and more Americans are world travelers in fact or via the printed page, to have at hand informed, insightful, and manageable literary guides to countries they may visit—or about which they "merely" seek to become knowledgeable—is very useful indeed. On several counts, then, we are in Johan Goudsblom's debt.

Charles H. Page

Santa Cruz, California

Preface

This book, it is hoped, will tell the reader something about Dutch society. Although much has been written about the Netherlands—there are many books dealing with its history, its landscape, its art, and its tourist attractions—so far, there has been no general sociological study of it as a contemporary society.

Writing about a specific national society raises many general problems of sociological theory and comparative analysis. In this study, I have chosen to avoid any explicit discussion of these matters in order not to depart from my particular subject: Dutch society. The emphasis is, in other words, descriptive rather than theoretical, on specific features of Dutch society rather than on general features of all societies.

Every description is incomplete. This is certainly true of a study that sets out to give, in so few pages, a survey

of a national society. Besides the size of the book, the
present limited state of empirical knowledge has often restricted the discussion. I have tried, however, to present
as much material as possible, ordered around the simple
themes of continuity and change and of unity and diversity. Hopefully, the references to other, more specialized
publications will compensate the reader for the inevitable
incompleteness. Wherever possible I refer to sources in
the English language.

The manuscript has benefited greatly from the advice
and criticism of several readers. Professor A. N. J. den
Hollander has generously given his encouragement and
critical support, Aad Nuis and Piet Nijhoff have taken a
continuously stimulating interest in the often faltering
progress of this study. Hans Daalder, Jos Lennards, Zvi
Namenwirth, and Cor E. Vervoort have given very helpful
assistance at various points.

Writing in a language that is not my own has often
presented me with difficulties. I was fortunate in receiving
many suggestions as to both substance and style from
Leon D. Bramson, Alan Curtis, Charles S. Fisher, John
H. Goldthorpe, and Peter I. Rose. I feel particularly in-
debted to Charles H. Page, whose thorough editorial work
has made this a better and more clearly written book.

                                                    J. G.

Princeton
May, 1966

Contents

DUTCH SOCIETY

{ I }

Introduction

A Distinct Nation

The Netherlands is a small country. Bounded by the North Sea on the West and North, by Germany on the East, and by Belgium on the South, it covers a land area of 12,850 square miles—about one fourth of the size of New York State. Within this territory live more than twelve million people, making the Netherlands one of the most densely populated countries in the world.

Owing to its location and its small size, the country has always been open to foreign influences. Historically the Netherlands belongs to European culture; in the past hundred years it has developed into a modern industrial country, sharing many typical features with other such countries, both in material conditions and in social organization. Today, influences from outside operate more strongly than ever before. Membership in the North Atlantic Treaty Organization and the European Common

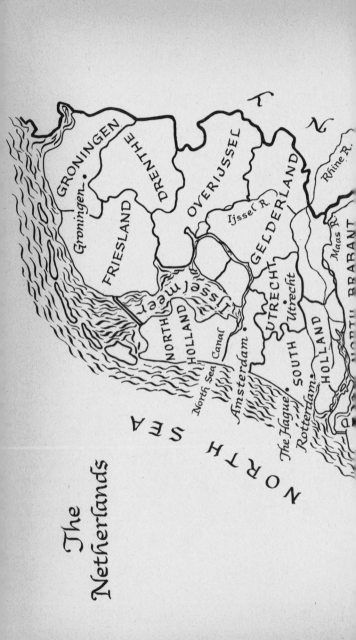

The Netherlands

Market entail political and economic cooperation on an international scale. Technical inventions from all over the world infuse the Dutch market and alter the Dutch way of life.

A visitor from any Western country, therefore, will recognize much in the Netherlands that is familiar to him. But he will also come across a great deal that is not quite the same as it would be elsewhere. The differences may often be hard to express exactly, yet they cannot possibly be denied: the landscape, the houses, the people are not just "Western" or "European"—they are Dutch. For centuries the national boundaries have operated as sieves, limiting contacts and influences from abroad.

No less than 96 per cent of the people living in the Netherlands today were born there,[1] and for most of them Dutch is their native tongue. All Dutch children attend the same type of elementary school, where they learn the same songs, stories, and rules of good behavior. In adult life, national institutions continue to affect people's activities in a great many situations. For everyone, there are national laws to obey, national taxes to pay, national holidays to celebrate. Thus, small though the country is, its national boundaries have real meaning: they mark a well-defined and to a large extent still self-contained social structure. As a result of growing up and living within these boundaries, almost every Dutchman acquires certain traits that reveal his nationality: his speech, his manners, and even his handwriting bear the stamp of Dutch culture.

Nation, Society, Social Structure, Culture

As a distinct social and cultural entity, the Netherlands can be called a nation and a society, but these two terms should not be treated as synonyms. In referring to the Netherlands as a nation, the emphasis here will be upon its existence as an integral unit amid other nations; the word "society" will stress the internal social and cultural structure. This distinction follows colloquial usage: it would sound awkward either to speak of the social stratification of a nation or to credit a person with feelings of loyalty toward his society, the latter concept being too diffuse to arouse identification.

As a society the Netherlands forms part of a much larger, vaguely circumscribed Western European, or Atlantic, or even world society. It is the nation that sets definite boundaries, demarcating the Dutch from the rest of the world. On the map we see the physical course of these boundaries; actually, of course, they are not merely of a physical but, more significantly, of a social and cultural nature. To a considerable extent, the national boundaries are evidenced by the activities of the government. Representing the Dutch people at the United Nations and in foreign capitals, negotiating and signing treaties, the government serves as a powerful intermediary between its citizens and the rest of the world. Other national organizations perform similar intermediary functions, in a more or less official fashion. National associations of many kinds— of science, commerce, sports, and so on—send delegations to international meetings and receive foreign delegations in turn. Special agencies acting as national "gatekeepers" manage the flow of goods and ideas to and from the Netherlands: import firms purchasing products from abroad and distributing these through domestic channels, communications media selecting and emitting international news, literary agents handling the translations of foreign books, and the like. In the present period of increasing international contacts, such national organizations of an intermediary character have gained in number and strength. Together, they represent the Dutch *nation* as a functioning unit.

Within this national framework we may conceive of Dutch *society* as a complex of social relationships and cultural institutions, some of which are organized at a national level, some at a regional or local level, and some hardly organized at all. In the most elementary sense the word "society," as Georg Simmel has pointed out, merely serves to indicate the fact that certain individuals are somehow "connected by interaction." [2] In the Netherlands, there are 12 million individuals—men and women, old and young, rich and poor, healthy and sick. Only one human variety is virtually lacking: the absolute hermit. All Dutchmen are in one way or another "connected by interaction" with other Dutchmen; consequently, almost anything they do or refrain from doing is somehow related to their being members of Dutch society. The time they get up in the morning is already largely determined by social conditions, and they remain enveloped in social situations for most of the day. The range of phenomena that might be subsumed under the label "Dutch society" appears to be endless. Outwardly at least they are confined within the boundaries set by the nation, but inwardly no limitations seem to exist: even in the spheres of utmost privacy and intimacy, "society" is still present.

The concepts of social structure and culture serve to help us map this bewildering variety of social facts. When studying people who are connected by interaction in a society, one may emphasize either their interpersonal relationships or their mutually shared ideas and habits. In speaking of *social structure,* we think primarily of the relationships between individuals and groups; in speaking of *culture,* we think primarily of the common ideas and habits that guide individual behavior. The distinction, it need

hardly be added, is by no means antithetical. Its useful-
ness lies in the fact that it enables us to separate conceptu-
ally such "structural" phenomena as social integration or
the existence of social classes from "cultural" systems like
language or religion. Eventually this conceptual separation may yield the empirical gain of establishing relationships between specific structural and cultural aspects of
society.

This, in brief, is the perspective we shall apply in dis-
cussing Dutch society. We shall be dealing with a nationally defined society, which will be described in terms of its
social structure and culture. How did this society origi-
nate, and to what extent are influences from the past still
at work? What are the main demographic factors differentiating the Dutch population? What, on the other hand,
are the main forces making for national integration? And
how does all this affect family and community life in the
Netherlands? These questions will be pivotal in the following chapters. In dealing with them, we hope to provide relevant information for readers interested in Dutch
society as such. There will be few new theoretical insights
in the pages that follow; they will contain largely the application of familiar concepts and principles to one specific
modern society.

Historical
Perspective

Dutch society is, and always has been, involved in processes of change. In recent years the population has been annually increasing by more than 1.2 per cent, the national income by more than 5.0 per cent. These small figures cover momentous changes, especially since the gains in both population and wealth have been unevenly distributed, affecting not only society as a whole but also the internal relations between its various segments. Any description of Dutch society is therefore time-bound, and will be out of date as change goes on. In order to correct these limitations as much as possible, we shall try to take account of the processes at work and to sort out some of the more lasting characteristics of Dutch society. What we need, then, is at least some measure of historical perspective.

Even such a seemingly unhistoric factor as geography

should be interpreted in the light of history. In the case of the Netherlands, this is particularly obvious, as borne out by the proverbial statement that "God made the world, but the Dutch made Holland." Indeed, a great deal of the physical landscape is literally man-made, about a third of the country consisting of former swamps, lakes, or even patches of sea drained one by one and turned into valuable *polder* land. To foreign observers the most striking feature of the Netherlands has always been the abundance of water: water constituting both a threat and a means of livelihood, necessitating the building of dams and dikes, and drawing the people toward seafaring and trade. Surely this factor of natural environment has provided an important stimulus; no less important, however, is the fact that the geographically favored occupations became feasible only at a time when their social and cultural prerequisites were fulfilled. Similarly, the discovery a few years ago of huge natural-gas deposits in the Netherlands, until then believed to be a country poorly endowed with natural resources, made dramatically clear again that the opportunities and challenges set by geography can be adequately assessed only in their relative historical significance.

If this is true of the country's physical features, it is even more true of its social and cultural characteristics: these are embedded in history. Before proceeding to discuss Dutch society of today, therefore, we shall present a brief historical perspective—first, by outlining some of the historical conditions under which the Dutch nation came into being, conditions that have had a lasting influence upon Dutch social structure and culture; and second, by sketching the main aspects of social change in its contemporary form as a process of modernization touching practically every facet of life in the Netherlands. Our historical interest does not aim at reconstructing the past "as it really was" but at enlightening the present. The selection of themes from history is guided by what we consider relevant for the development of the nation until the present time, and not by what once may have been felt to be of utmost importance.

The Origin of the Nation

The Dutch nation owes its existence to a set of specific historical circumstances. There are no natural boundaries separating the Netherlands from neighboring Belgium and Germany; nor do the Dutch people possess any clearly evident physical characteristics that set them apart from other peoples in Western Europe. Not even linguistically is the Netherlands a clear-cut unit: The Dutch language has developed out of a Germanic branch of the Indo-European family; to the south it extends well into Belgium, and on the east the official Dutch-German language border meanders through local dialects which even today can often be hardly distinguished.

There are several words in use to refer to the country and its inhabitants: the Netherlands, Holland, the Dutch. In contrast to this profusion is the fact that the two "low countries," Belgium and the Netherlands, both have provinces called Brabant and Limburg. Such verbal inconsistencies bear witness to the mixed historical origins of the Dutch nation. In the Middle Ages the region now covered by the Netherlands and Belgium was divided into a large number of duchies, counties, and bishoprics, whose feudal lords exercised practically sovereign rights. After 1384 the ducal House of Burgundy managed to unify most of these principalities into one realm. It did not establish a national state, however, but only a personal union of territories, each of which kept its own laws and privileges.

The emergence of the Dutch nation from this loosely

fragmented realm can be dated rather precisely as having occurred in the last decades of the sixteenth century.[1] By that time the Burgundians had been succeeded by the Hapsburg family, whose reign, based upon conquest and marriage, extended as far as Spain and the Spanish-American colonies. The vastness of this empire created continuous conflicts between the dynasty and the leading representatives of the low countries. The heavy financial demands made on behalf of remote wars met with persistent opposition. When in the 1560s the king levied a general sales tax, promoted Spanish noblemen to the highest offices, and enforced the rule of the Inquisition as a tool of central power, these absolutist impositions called forth unrest, protest, and finally outright revolt. Initially, all the Netherlandish provinces took part in the revolt; but while it succeeded in the North, it failed in the South. As a result, the northern half became an independent republic from which the Dutch nation was to emerge, whereas the southern half, Belgium, remained a Hapsburg dominion, not to gain independence until the nineteenth century.

This was a result unforeseen and unintended. The revolt that brought freedom to the North had actually started in the South. Once it was under way, many reasons prompted people to join: "privileges, ancient customs, fair taxation, toleration and religious freedom, democracy for some, the mastery of their own class for others."[2] Military events eventually settled the outcome: the Spanish troops always operated from the South, where they had their bases; thanks to a strategic position amid sea and lakes, Holland and Zeeland in the North could hold out until bankruptcy and mutiny forced the Spanish commanders to give up. The territory remaining outside the Spanish lines after the last big campaign in 1585 housed the center of the victorious Republic. Those regions which Dutch generals conquered in the following years were added to the territory of the Republic, but they remained devoid of the rights possessed by the other provinces: designated as "lands of the generality," the territories of North Brabant and Limburg received neither regional autonomy nor the right of delegation to the central government at The Hague.

The American historian John L. Motley has compared the Dutch struggle for independence with that of the United States.[3] Both were directed against a distant government whose representatives were regarded as foreigners. Neither was an actual revolution in the sense that an existing government was overthrown and replaced by a new one. Instead, both were separation movements, proclaiming a new sovereign state. Similarities also obtain for some of the key issues the new states had to face. Thus, in both cases a crisis of legitimacy had to be met; in the Netherlands the charismatic leadership of William of Orange and a vindication of traditional privileges played an important part.[4]

Altogether, the rise of the Dutch nation was not guided by any preconceived plan. The first years of independence in the North brought a great deal of hesitation and confusion, until finally the Repubic of the Seven United Provinces was founded, a confederation comprising Holland, Zeeland, Friesland, Groningen, Overijsel, Gelderland, and Utrecht. Within this Republic, which was primarily a political union, national institutions developed and a sense of national identity emerged. By the beginning of the seventeenth century, the Dutch nation as a distinct social and cultural unit was well established—in the experience of its own citizens as well as in the recognition of foreigners. Within a few decades the new nation rapidly rose to great economic prosperity, political power, and cultural splendor. The "need for payoff" contingent upon any new political establishment[5] was amply met with the aid of the commercial successes of the state-supported East Indies Company. In the arts and sciences the seventeenth century, because of such men as Rembrandt, Huyghens, Grotius, and Spinoza, still stands out as the golden age of Dutch history.

Consolidation: A Commonwealth of Burghers

Several features characteristic of the Dutch state in its first years were to have an enduring impact upon nation and society. To begin with, the state was highly decentralized. According to what is usually regarded as its founding charter, the Union of Utrecht (1579), the seven provinces remained sovereign "allies," each of which sent its own delegates to the federal assembly, the States-General in The Hague. This assembly, with its nominally sovereign constituents, could make decisions only by unanimous vote. Arrangements, on the whole, allowed for a great deal of regional autonomy: Such matters as jurisdiction and taxation rested almost entirely with provincial authority. As a result, many regional differences in social structure and culture remained more or less unaffected by national influences. For example, whereas the coastal provinces of Holland and Zeeland were dominated by a class of rich city merchants, the landed gentry managed to maintain a powerful feudal position in the inland rural regions of Gelderland and Overijsel. Regional diversity remained even greater among the lower social strata, where people were only indirectly involved in national affairs.

Although the seven provinces were nominally of equal status, in effect one of them carried by far the most power. It is not by chance that even today the whole country is often referred to as "Holland": all during the history of the Republic, until its final breakup in 1795, Holland was the unchallenged political and economic leader of the nation. Each year it contributed 58 per cent of the federal budget—enough to settle any major dispute. Holland's wealth derived from shipping; its interests were on the sea, not the land. This maritime orientation of its foremost province was carried over into the policies of the Republic as a whole. In continental European politics its main concern was the preservation of a balance of power that would guarantee Dutch independence. Hardly ever did it seek to expand its territories east or south; of far greater importance was the foundation of colonial strongholds all over the world. The overseas conquests and settlements, especially in the Dutch East Indies, contributed a great deal to Dutch wealth and power as well as to the national self-image and national self-esteem.[6]

Within the dominant province of Holland, political and economic power rested almost exclusively with a comparatively small elite of rich merchants and their kin. It was they who controlled shipping and finance and who for many successive generations formed a self-contained oligarchy, sharing almost all important public offices among its own members. Historians have variously described them as patricians, city magnates, and burgher aristocrats; the names by which they were best known in their own time were "regents" (*regenten*) or simply "gentlemen" (*heeren*). It is impossible to measure exactly the impact their reign has had upon Dutch society. Much, however, that strikes one today as "typically Dutch" can plausibly be traced back to the fact that in its first centuries the Dutch nation had as its leading elite a rich and haughty patriciate, acting in self-appointed authority as superordinate trustees of the people. The older cities still preserve alongside their canals long rows of stately mansions in which the rich burgher families expressed their wealth and prestige; in the side streets smaller houses of the same design show how the model was imitated by the less affluent. In contrast, the absence in Dutch architecture of monumental layouts indicates in a negative way that the tone was set by an elite averse to military grandeur or courtly splendor. At a more intangible level, a certain forthrightness and lack of courtesy in manners appear to reflect the same tradition.

Similarly difficult to assess, but probably of no less import, has been the effect of the Reformation, and notably of Calvinism, upon Dutch society. The advent of Calvinism in the Netherlands coincided with the rising tide of revolt against Spain. From the very start it served the cause of the rebellion as a source of inspiration and justification. Although its adherents in these early years did not number more than 5 per cent of the population, their militant fervor and tough organization put them in the vanguard of the revolt. As the northern provinces gained independence, the Calvinists, utilizing the power of the newly founded state, set out to mold the people into a Protestant nation. They managed to take charge of the schools, to make membership in the Dutch Reformed Church a prerequisite for appointment to civic office, and to forbid by law all public religious worship outside this same church. Again, the last decades of the sixteenth century proved to be formative years: The regions then controlled by the young Republic were by and large protestantized, while in the remaining territories the Counter-Reformation, supported by the Spanish forces, launched a successful campaign of recatholicization. Today the geographic distribution of Protestants and Roman Catholics still follows in broad outline the boundaries of the Republic in the late sixteenth century. A number of substantial enclaves of Catholicism in the North reflect the enduring accomplishments of those priests who stood their ground in that crucial period.

Although Calvinism made strong headway in the

emergent Dutch state and nation, it never won over the entire population, nor did it gain complete political control. Even one of the first constitutional drafts of the Republic (1579) stated that "no one may be prosecuted or investigated in the cause of religion." In spite of some violations, this principle of religious freedom for the individual became a tenet of the Republic. The Dutch Reformed Church remained the only religious organization that was officially recognized. The minorities of Roman Catholics, Protestant dissenters, and Jews suffered some discrimination, especially in being ineligible for public office; they were tolerated, however, and although it was against the law, they were usually allowed to conduct their worship without restrictions. Within the official church itself there was a continuous tension between the "true" orthodox Calvinists, who insisted upon stringent observation of doctrine and the moderates, who held a more worldly and liberal point of view. The orthodox faction, led by the ministers, had a large following among the common people; the latitudinarian attitude prevailed among the leading merchant-regents. Contrary to Max Weber's well-known thesis, the latter category as a whole stood rather aloof from radical Calvinism.[7] Their commercial interests were better served by peace and tolerance than by theological zealotry. They therefore provided a powerful counterweight to Calvinist dominance and created a social climate favorable to freedom of thought, for which the Dutch Republic was famous throughout the seventeenth and eighteenth centuries. As a result, Dutch society, besides offering sanctuary to many foreign refugees, could preserve a varied religious composition among its native population.

From the beginning of the seventeenth century, three distinct major religious groups existed side by side in the Netherlands: the orthodox Calvinists, representing the official Dutch Reformed Church, strict in doctrine and convinced of their religious superiority; the moderate Protestants, less interested in theological matters but often prominent in political and economic life; and the Roman Catholics, who had practically no part in national affairs but still comprised a sizable portion of the population. The lines drawn by this threefold division have left an almost indelible imprint upon Dutch society.

Aspects of Modernization

The conditions of its origin in the late sixteenth century have given a particular twist to the further social and cultural development of the Dutch nation. For the whole period up to the French Revolution, it remained "an amazing laboratory of social history," [8] uniquely advanced in being a Republic led by an elite of burghers, yet archaic in harboring many survivals of medieval regionalism. Since the nineteenth century, however, Dutch society has come to be increasingly involved in a general process of modernization whose impetus mostly originated elsewhere, a process that has tended to reduce the singularity of the indigenous social structure and culture.

During the Napoleonic era the Netherlands experienced its first foreign occupation since the defeat of Spain. This episode brought a decisive break in the nation's political history, notably in the effect of greater centralization: The provinces lost their sovereignty, the territories of North Brabant and Drente at last attained equal status with the other provinces, a uniform civil and penal code was drawn up for the whole country, and taxation was similarly standardized. At the end of the war the Congress of Vienna forged the Netherlands and Belgium into one kingdom, headed by the House of Orange. The reunion proved unsatisfactory; the two peoples had grown too far apart, and they separated again in 1830. The frontiers of the Netherlands have not undergone any substantial change since. As a constitutional monarchy, the Dutch state now possessed a stronger central authority than the Republic ever had; yet regional variety remained great, especially in the rural areas. The domination of Holland over the other provinces continued to only a slightly lesser degree, and within Holland the city elites maintained their leading positions. The predominant spiritual outlook was still Protestant with liberal tendencies; the orthodox Calvinists found themselves rather more out of touch with political power than before; and the Roman Catholics played only a very minor part on the national scene.

By the mid-nineteenth century, the Netherlands had about 3 million inhabitants. The bulk of the population still lived in rural communities and pursued an agrarian economy. The nation's most important source of wealth was foreign trade, especially with the East Indian colonies: the tropical products coffee and sugar far surpassed the agrarian home produce in the Dutch export market, while the contribution of industry was negligible. The profits of foreign trade went for the most part to the merchants. The burgher class strongly dominated the political and economic scene; in social relations it sustained a rigid system of subtle distinctions. The majority of the people were economically poor, politically powerless, socially subordinate, and culturally unenlightened. Women, regardless of their social class, had no political and but few economic rights. Only in the upper layers of society did some national organizations exist; the great majority of people lived most of their lives in local or regional isolation. Standards of hygiene and sanitation were low as compared with today, and the average life expectancy at birth only just exceeded 30 years.

Such was the general picture in the middle of the nineteenth century. From our present point of view several details may strike us as typical of an "underdeveloped" condition. The analogy should not be stressed too far, but in a way it may also be illuminating. Around 1850 Dutch society was rather stagnant and slow to catch up with changes that were already taking place in surrounding countries. The prevailing pattern of life was traditional; members of the leading classes cultivated a complacent disdain of "progress." Construction of the first railroads, for example, had to be financed largely by foreign capital and carried out by foreign technicians; among Dutchmen there was a widespread feeling that in a country so well accommodated with waterways as theirs the steam locomotive could never compete with the horsedrawn boat, the *trekschuit*.[9] The atmosphere was neatly epitomized by one *trekschuit*-traveler, the German poet Heinrich Heine, in his remark that if the world should perish he would go to the Netherlands: there everything happened fifty years later.

It is impossible to date exactly when the social climate altered and the process of modernization began. The very word "modernization" is a relative term that refers to a complex of processes with a particular direction rather than to an event with a fixed beginning and end. But one thing is certain: Dutch society began rather late to move in this direction, and the movement did not gain real momentum until the second half of the nineteenth century. Once the processes had got under way, they were to transform the Netherlands into a modern industrial society. In several instances the impact of modernization can be clearly demonstrated by figures. Thus, between 1850 and 1965 the average life expectancy at birth rose from 30 to 72 years. In the same period the population surged from 3 to 12 million, a 400 per cent increase. In spite of this growth, the net income per capita grew at least 250 per cent, while the average amount of leisure time more than doubled.[10]

A prime factor underlying these changes has been the process of *mechanization*, the replacement of human and animal energy by steam, gas, and electricity. Since the late Middle Ages, windmills had been a valuable asset to the Dutch economy, but the net energy they produced averaged only about 15 horsepower. The new inventions of the steam engine, the electric generator, and the internal combustion engine multiplied the potential supply of energy almost beyond comparison. These devices could be readily introduced in the Netherlands, thanks to the availability of sufficient capital and technical skill. As elsewhere, they have greatly reduced man's immediate dependence upon nature, but at the same time they have heightened his reliance upon a complicated social apparatus without which the benefits of mechanization cannot be had.

An important part in the creation of this apparatus has been played by *industrialization*. The generation of mechanical energy and its application to production usually require big plants. In 1850 the Netherlands possessed only one factory with a thousand employees; today there are well over a hundred. The two largest industrial corporations in Western Europe, Unilever and Shell, are joint British-Dutch companies; in addition, the Netherlands is the home of several other industrial giants with interests all over the world. Large-scale industry has changed the landscape of the country and the economic and social structure of Dutch society. It has drawn an increasing proportion of the working population within its orbit; the agrarian sector has been declining steadily, and is already less than 10 per cent of the labor force.

If in its technical aspects industrialization presupposes

mechanization, socially it is closely identified with an intricate division of labor, or *specialization*. Anyone working in an industrial plant has a specific task to fulfill; internal specialization is a basic principle of the factory system. Moreover, since the factory system is likely to produce almost any commodity with greater efficiency than could be achieved by individual effort, it impels the entire population to engage in similarly specialized economic tasks. The farm household where most daily needs are met by the family's own labor suffers a definite disadvantage as compared with the specialized industries catering to specific demands. Consequently, specialization has entered the agrarian as well as the industrial sector; the highly developed enterprise of bulb growing is a well-known example.

Today's Dutch bulb-growers owe their worldwide success not merely to the natural qualities of their soil, but also to the rational application of scientific findings and the careful calculation of risks, costs, and profits. This brings to the fore the process of *rationalization* as an important aspect of modernization: the increasing tendency to rely on reason rather than on tradition or chance. By this we do not mean that the entire process of modernization has been the outcome of rational planning, nor that today all Dutch people have developed into wholly rational beings incapable of unpremeditated action. Yet it is true that the social and cultural environment they live in is in many ways the result of rational deliberations. The highly efficient system of health organizations which has gradually been built up is a manifest example of how rationalization has pervaded Dutch society and altered—in this case prolonged—people's lives.

Rationalization has been particularly effective in the form of *bureaucratization*, the rise of large, internally specialized and hierarchically ordered administrative organizations. No more than any of the other processes mentioned is bureaucratization a wholly novel phenomenon, but its rapid advance is a typical aspect of modernization. One index of bureaucratization is the increase of white-collar civil servants; between 1900 and 1950 their numbers increased more than eightfold (from 20,000 to 165,000), while the total Dutch working population approximately doubled.[11] In the same period industrial corporations, banks, insurance companies, trade unions, and many other organizations have contributed to the further expansion of bureaucracy.

Bureaucratization has facilitated *centralization*, the tendency to submit local or regional autonomy to a central authority. In the past century almost every field of social activity has witnessed successful efforts at centralization, either under government auspices or by voluntary association. A hundred years ago social welfare depended entirely upon local initiatives; today it is basically regulated by national legislation. In quite another area, both government price control and the various commercial cartels represent instances of centralization. Although the process has been most obvious at the national level, it is also reflected at lower levels in ubiquitous attempts at regulations and coordination, such as fixing closing hours and holidays for shops.

The process of centralization has impaired the former autonomy of cities. No longer are city councils free to raise their own finances and to manage their own affairs as they see fit. Yet, although in this way modernization has been detrimental to the political life of cities, it has greatly stimulated their economic prosperity and their numerical growth. Ever since the Middle Ages cities had flourished in the Netherlands, especially in the province of Holland. Amsterdam, in particular, had long been one of the most prominent cities in Europe, famous for its wealth and its well-planned spatial layout.[12] Still, around 1850 its population numbered only 225,000, and no other Dutch city had over 100,000 inhabitants. In the decades that followed, a rapid growth set in, due first of all to the general growth of the population and more specifically to such trends as the concentration of labor in big industries, the rise of bureaucratic organizations, and the proliferation of specialized trades and professions. Today there are fourteen cities of more than 100,000 inhabitants, totaling more than three and a half million people, or almost one-third of the Dutch population.

The available census figures, however, do not quite measure the entire process of *urbanization*. They fail to reveal the infusion of urban elements into the rural way of life, a process so close to urbanization that it has been called "rurbanization." Again, the neologism does not refer to a phenomenon that is altogether new. Ever since the Middle Ages, the Dutch cities have exerted cultural influences upon their agrarian surroundings. The process of diffusion had always been slow, however, allowing time for the new to become assimilated with the traditional. Consequently, around 1850 most rural regions still preserved a marked individuality expressed in speech, dress, and folklore. During the past century such distinctive characteristics have tended to disappear as the effects of modernization have penetrated into even the most isolated areas. The few communities where visible manifestations of traditional culture survived are now increasingly capitalizing upon these relics for the commercial profits of tourism.

In a way the opening up of rural society forms part of the more general process of *democratization*. This process has been most evident in the political sphere. Around 1850, only 10 per cent of male Dutch citizens had the right to vote. In the next seventy years, the groups that had been excluded were gradually enfranchised: the artisans and shopkeepers, the farmers, the wage workers, and last of all, the women. By 1919, universal suffrage was established. The developing democratic system drew leaders from formerly unrepresented categories to positions of national importance, thus broadening the social basis of the nation's political elite. Along with political emancipation has gone an increasing social participation and cultural elevation of large segments of the population. The social handicap of illiteracy virtually disappeared after the introduction of compulsory school education in 1901.

Thus a series of processes has contributed to the general trend of modernization that has been and still is transforming Dutch society. These processes are all intricately connected; every step in each process began from the cumulative effects of all processes together. The list we have given is incomplete; for example, it does not explicitly mention any changes within the family. In order to convey the significance of the transformation, we have included only some of the most obvious large-scale trends, whose impact can be demonstrated by statistical evidence for the nation as a whole. Modernization has been no less effective at the level of individual roles and values. Those changes are far more difficult to measure, but it should be clear that the personal life of every Dutchman is embedded in a social and cultural environment that is continuously in flux.

More often than not the causes of modernization lay far beyond the Netherlands. As David Riesman remarked, "Modernization appears to proceed with an almost irreversible impact, and no tribe or nation has found a place to hide." [13] In this sense the modernization of Dutch society has been a process of acculturation to a rapidly changing world environment. Its effects have been mainly to create greater similarities between the Netherlands and other modern nations. Yet, although the past fifteen years have shown modernization to be making faster strides than ever before, we have not yet reached a stage of global or even continental uniformity. Dutch society still displays some rather specific features.

The Indigenous and the Modern

Our perspective so far has pointed in two directions: toward some historically developed characteristics typical of Dutch society on the one hand, and toward a series of processes operating in modern industrial society at large on the other. Still lacking in our survey is the confrontation of these two aspects, showing how the process of modernization has affected the older indigenous social and cultural patterns. Regional variety, the hegemony of Holland, a merchant elite, strong Calvinistic tendencies, and religious differentiation—these had been distinctive features of the Dutch Republic during its entire history up until 1795. How have these characteristics sustained the advance of modernity?

In order to answer this question it seems useful to focus upon one common element in such diverse processes as industrialization, bureaucratization, centralization, urbanization and democratization: they all imply the formation of larger social entities. Industrialization brings together great numbers of employees within a single factory; it indirectly generates such organizations as trade unions and consumer associations. Each in their own way, the other processes have a similar effect of establishing new social relationships, of drawing formerly distant segments of the population closer together. The social network grows denser; the members of society become more interdependent and involved in mutual and common ties. In other words, new forms of social integration arise. This trend has been most obvious at the national level. There has been a proliferation of national organizations for all sorts of activities and, concurrently, a growing national orientation on the part of the people concerned. In general it can be said that for the past century Dutch society has shown an *increasing national integration of social structure* and, along with this, an *increasing acceptance of a common national culture* by all its members.[14]

This trend obviously runs counter to the maintenance of regional autonomy and isolation. The social and cultural characteristics of different parts of the country have tended toward greater uniformity. In most areas landscape and architecture still preserve the distinctive regional style of past generations, but the more recent additions tend to be more or less the same all over the country. Besides being visible in the material culture, the effects of national integration are also audible in the decline of local dialects. Again, traditional differences have not yet completely disappeared, but they are diminishing rapidly: "Many a funeral in the countryside means the interment of an idiom." [15] In many villages in the province of Friesland, the original Frisian language is still used as the language of everyday life. Here too, however, national influences make themselves strongly felt. Every Frisian child has to learn Dutch upon entering school, so that Frisian has become a typical modern minority language, spoken only by bilinguals. A sense of patriotic pride, based upon a tradition dating back to the first centuries A.D., is still shared by many Frisians, but this pride is more the nostalgic memory of an ancient past than an active desire to be different today.[16] As far as general regional differences go, the most notable distinction in contemporary Dutch society is that between the southern provinces of North Brabant and Limburg and the rest of the country. Although the traditional disparities have been smoothed out to a considerable degree, these two provinces continue to show signs of forming a separate "subculture." [17]

The dominance of Holland has also declined but not disappeared. Today the three central western provinces of North Holland, South Holland, and Utrecht still combine the greatest density of population and the highest income per capita. The best-known museums, theaters, and concert halls are concentrated in this same area. No less significantly, the entire nation still bears the economic seal of the district of Holland in its heavy reliance upon foreign trade; the total value of imports and exports in relation to national income is higher in the Netherlands than in any other Western European country. To a large extent the national integration of formerly isolated regional groups has meant their assimilation to institutions set by Holland.

If in this last sentence "Holland" is read as a geographical term, then a sociological connotation must be added: The dominant reference group in the process of assimilation has been Holland's elite, the affluent and powerful burghers. It was they who first established a nationwide network of administration and trade; as successively more segments of the population began to take an active part in this network, they tended to adopt the standards of behavior that had already been set by the bourgeois elite. This is borne out by the almost undisputed recognition of a national standard language, a language directly derived from the usage of the leading circles in Amsterdam and a few other cities in Holland. Today school education and mass media expose the entire population to this linguistic standard; adjustment to it is almost indispensable for social ascent above a local level.[18]

Besides the rules of language, many other models have diffused from the burgher elite to society at large, models covering a wide range of conduct from table manners to standards of cleanliness, personal bearing, and sexual morality. An important characteristic of the bourgeois standards of speech and etiquette is that they generally encourage "civility," that is, conduct which never indulges in an open display of emotions, but conceals the actor's innermost feelings behind a restrained observance of conventional forms. Obviously, such conduct is particularly appropriate to those social contexts in which to be in "command of oneself" is an important asset in order to "command the situation." The spread of bourgeois civility as a cultural trait can therefore be explained partly on structural grounds. The rich merchants were the first social group in the Netherlands to have regular and frequent contacts with a great variety of people in a specifically businesslike setting. These contacts usually involved the individual in only one capacity; his private affairs were deliberately treated as irrelevant, and care was taken to suppress all extreme utterances of surprise, anger, or joy. Instead, he cultivated a kind of conduct that established mutual confidence and *rapport,* while at the same time preserving distance and avoiding intimacy. Thus the rules of civility, offering standardized modes of presenting oneself in an appropriately reserved manner, were developed. In addition, and no less importantly, civility also represented prestige and recognition: like the proper clothing, it was a way to prove one's identity as a respectable and well-educated person. This prestige function of civil conduct has sometimes called forth resistance, especially in socialist quarters; nevertheless, in practically every national organization, including the labor party and labor unions, the dominant code of behavior is civil: Civility appears to present a generally acceptable set of rules for the kind of relationships that sustain a nationally integrated social structure.[19]

The process of national integration has widened the

scope of contacts between different regions and between different socioeconomic classes. In addition, it has drawn formerly isolated religious groupings closer together, both in cooperation and in conflict. One of the most striking features of the modernization of Dutch society has been the fact that the two most important religious minorities, the orthodox Calvinists and the Roman Catholics, were the first to launch a successful emancipation movement some decades before the working classes began to respond to the call of socialism. The immediate cause prompting the religious minorities to action lay in a series of measures initiated in the middle of the nineteenth century, measures by which the ruling liberal bourgeoisie intended to further general education upon a secular basis. Against these attempts Calvinist as well as Roman Catholic leaders insisted upon school instruction with a religious background. Throughout the second half of the century the "school struggle" remained one of the dividing issues in Dutch politics. As the franchise was gradually extended in the interim, national parties and leagues were founded which rallied the voters with an appeal to religious principles. Thus the scene was set for a process of "segmented integration" whereby several blocs of the population, defined by their religion or *Weltanschauung,* strove for fuller participation in society. When toward the end of the century socialism emerged as a political force, it joined the already existing pattern as a full-fledged ideological bloc. The liberal bourgeoisie that had originally controlled national affairs was increasingly forced into an equal position with the newly founded blocs. Although even today the liberals still like to cling to the epithet "general" in describing themselves, in effect they have come to constitute another bloc, characterized ideologically by their de-emphasis of either religious denomination or social class in political matters.

The ensuing situation is known in Dutch as *verzuiling*, which means literally "columnization" or "pillarization," the idea being that the various blocs of the population represent separate "pillars" (*zuilen*), each valuable in its own right, and together indispensable in supporting the national structure. The phenomenon of *verzuiling* is by no means confined to politics. Each denominational bloc has set up a whole array of organizations encompassing practically every sphere of social life. Schools and universities, radio and television corporations, trade unions, health and welfare agencies, sport associations, and so on, all fit into the *zuilen* system. The actual number of blocs represented may vary in different areas, depending upon special alliances; the usual division is fourfold, between a Calvinist, a Roman Catholic, a "general," and a socialist bloc. The latter two may sometimes be combined to form a sort of "antibloc," or they may be accompanied by yet another bloc of latitudinarian Protestants. We shall come across several manifestations of *verzuiling* in the following pages; here we only want to indicate the phenomenon as resulting from the interaction of traditional religious diversity and the modernizing process of national integration.[20]

It has sometimes been alleged that the "totalitarian" tendencies of Calvinism have been the primary cause of the segmentation of Dutch society.[21] This interpretation does not sufficiently acknowledge the combined impact of Calvinism and Roman Catholicism as two already existing molds within which large parts of the population attained fuller participation in national life, guided by their own leaders. Many observers have noted a particular Calvinistic streak in the Dutch national character, an impression that is hard to prove but is plausible. The etiquette of civil relationships, although basically similar, varies in details from one society to another. The Dutch case is marked by a tendency not to overdo civility: in manners, neither elegance nor modesty is greatly cultivated. In part this may be ascribed to the heritage of the self-conscious regent elite, which found little occasion to go out of its way in politeness to anybody, but it may have been equally important that this example was reinforced in the lower strata of society by the teachings of Calvinism, instilling a distrust of extravagance and encouraging sobriety.

Dutch society today shows several other features that reflect the typical manner in which national integration has developed. Thus, political arrangements are marked by a multiparty system firmly rooted in the *zuilen* system. As a result of the deep involvement of political parties in the all-embracing divisions of *verzuiling,* election returns have tended to be very stable throughout the years. Another notable feature has been the comparatively low frequency of strikes; in the nineteen fifties the relative number of working days lost in this way was by far the lowest in Western Europe. It is likely that behind this record of peace on the labor front lies an ethic of responsibility shared by the various blocs, each of which has a stake in the prevailing social order. Demographic statistics also reveal a phenomenon unique in Western Europe: an annual birth rate that never dropped below 19 per thousand inhabitants, not even during the economic depression of the nineteen thirties. This fact appears to indicate that by and large Dutch society has not undergone an abrupt break with tradition. In this respect the *zuilen* system may have served as a mitigating factor, restraining the social and cultural impact of modernization.

Such speculations, however, anticipate more detailed treatment. In concluding this historical introduction to Dutch society as a whole, we wish to emphasize once more that in the nineteenth and twentieth centuries, this society has become increasingly susceptible to international trends and events. Some of the main trends have already been noted. As for the principal historical events, we would mention only the Great Depression and the Second World War.[22] Both have thoroughly affected Dutch society; yet in their threat to the established order, they have also brought out the tenacity of some lasting elements in Dutch social structure and culture.

{ III }

Demographic Composition and Social Differentiation

The preceding chapter presented a historical perspective of Dutch society as a whole: how it originated, how it acquired an identity of its own, and how it has been absorbing the impact of modernization. Before continuing our discussion of Dutch society as a functioning unit, it will be useful to examine more closely the composition of its population. For, although all Dutchmen are in some way involved in the nation's social structure and culture, the kind and extent of this involvement vary a great deal. A biography of the "typical Dutchman" is almost inconceivable: too many vital details would have to be left out. In this chapter we shall try to fill in some of these details for several social categories. Our purpose will be, in other words, to provide the main "personalia" of different segments of the Dutch population.

In small nonliterate societies, the chief determinants of

an individual's social and cultural participation are age, sex, kinship, and residence. In the much larger national society of the Netherlands, age, sex, and residence still constitute important social and cultural differentials. Instead of kinship, however, we shall discuss two other significant personal attributes, religion and socioeconomic status. Racial and ethnic factors of great importance in many modern societies play a very minor role in the Netherlands, and will be mentioned only in passing.

Birth and Death Rates

Like all modern industrial societies, Dutch society is undergoing a sizable change in its age composition. Each year statistics reveal a relative decrease of the young and an increase of the adult and the aged in the total population. As elsewhere, the causes of this shift lie in a continuous lowering of both the birth and the death rates: Fewer children are born per family and people live longer. Thanks to a systematic application of medical and hygienic care, the Netherlands boasts one of the lowest death rates in the world. The progress made in the past century is impressive. In 1870 the average life expectancy at birth was 38.4 years for men and 40.7 for women; by the turn of the century it had risen to 51.0 and 53.4, respectively; today these figures are 71.4 and 74.8. As a result, "the average inhabitant of the Netherlands of today witnesses in his family-circle only one quarter of the number of deaths that his ancestors a few generations ago experienced in their lifetime." [1]

Whereas the Dutch death rate has followed a more or less "normal" pattern, the birth rate has deviated so much from developments elsewhere that it has been called "a demographic anomaly." [2] As in other European countries, fertility has declined throughout the twentieth century,

TABLE 1

Crude Birth Rates per 1,000 Population for Eight
Western European Countries, 1910–1961

Years	Countries							
	Netherlands	Denmark	Norway	Sweden	England	Belgium	France	Switzerland
1910–11	28.2	27.1	25.4	24.4	24.8	23.3	19.2	24.6
1920–21	28.2	24.7	25.3	22.6	24.0	22.0	21.1	20.9
1928–29	23.1	19.1	17.6	15.7	16.5	18.5	18.0	17.3
1938–39	20.6	18.0	15.6	15.2	15.0	15.8	14.9	15.2
1950–51	22.5	18.2	18.8	16.0	15.7	16.7	20.2	17.7
1955–56	21.3	17.3	18.5	14.8	15.4	16.8	18.6	17.3
1960–61	21.0	16.6	17.4	13.8	17.3	17.0	18.2	17.9

SOURCE: Netherlands Central Bureau of Statistics, quoted by F. van Heek, "Het Nederlandse geboortepatroon en de godsdienstfactor gedurende de laatste halve eeuw," *Mens en Maatschappij*, XXXVIII (1963), 85.

with only a temporary recovery in the years following the Second World War. As shown in Table 1, however, this decline has not made up for the initial excess manifested at the beginning of the century. Consequently, although the proportion of young people has decreased steadily, it is still rather high in comparison with most other European countries.

Here is one of the peculiar features of Dutch society, the causes of which are most likely to be found in its specific historical background. Two leading Dutch sociologists, E. W. Hofstee and F. van Heek, have paid particular attention to different historical aspects of the problem. According to Hofstee, we are dealing with the same process of birth decline that has been operating in all other countries of Western Europe; the Netherlands is unique only because this process has had a relatively late start there, especially in the southern and eastern regions. Van Heek, on the other hand, has drawn attention to the differential birth rates of various religious categories; he attaches primary significance to the historic position of Roman Catholics in Dutch society. Although the authors have on occasion criticized each other's view, it seems that actually the two interpretations can be taken as complementary.[3]

An important contribution of Hofstee has been to modify the familiar transition model in demography which postulates the historical sequence of (1) high birth and death rates, (2) high birth and low death rates, and (3) both low birth and low death rates.[4] In the middle of the nineteenth century, when the impact of modernization was only mildly felt, the Netherlands still showed the traditional combination of a high birth and a high death rate (see Table 2). Few if any families practiced direct birth control; yet in an indirect manner, through postponement and restriction of marriage, limits were set to the actual

TABLE 2

Crude Birth and Death Rates per 1,000 Population for
the Netherlands, 1849–1964

Year	Birth Rate	Death Rate	Natural Increase
1849	33.8	25.5	8.3
1859	35.2	24.8	10.4
1869	36.2	24.5	11.7
1879	34.7	21.3	13.4
1889	32.7	18.7	14.0
1899	31.0	15.7	15.3
1909	29.2	13.7	15.5
1919	24.4	13.4	11.0
1929	22.8	10.7	12.1
1939	20.6	8.6	12.0
1949	23.7	8.1	15.6
1959	21.4	7.6	13.8
1960	20.8	7.6	13.2
1961	21.3	7.6	13.7
1962	20.9	8.0	12.9
1963	20.9	8.0	12.9
1964	20.7	7.7	13.0

SOURCES: For 1849–1899, William Petersen, *Planned Migration* (Berkeley: University of California Press, 1955), p. 28; for 1900–1949, Centraal Bureau voor de Statistiek, *Zestig jaren statistiek in tijdreeksen* (Zeist: W. de Haan, 1959), pp. 13–15; for 1959–1964, Centraal Bureau voor de Statistiek, *Statistisch Zakboek 1965* (Hilversum: W. de Haan, 1965), p. 11.

number of births. During the third quarter of the nineteenth century, as the death rate was already declining, the birth rate rose to an unprecedented maximum of 37.1 in 1877. This rise in natality has not been accounted for in the conventional model of demographic transition. Hofstee calls it the "proletarian phase" following the breakup of traditional communities and notably of the extended family as the unit of working and living. As traditional restrictions fell away, the number of marriages increased considerably. Since birth control within the family was still largely absent, this resulted in a heightened birth rate. Only after 1880 did the rising line of natality bend back toward a general decline that was to continue with but minor interruptions until the present day. The decline marked the beginning of the modern "rational" family phase, characterized by few restrictions on marriage and a spreading practice of deliberate birth control within the family.

By and large the changes in both natality and mortality have occurred first in the western and northern parts of the country and only later in the East and South. Hofstee attributes this to the spread of the "modern dynamic pattern of culture," which supposedly determines people's willingness to adopt innovations. As the favorable attitude toward change advances, Hofstee predicts, the regional differences in birth and death rates will tend to disappear. Already the tables have been turned in that the western provinces, although still having a far lower birth rate than the southern, are showing a slight rise in natality, whereas in the South the decline continues. The expectation seems warranted, therefore, that Dutch society as a whole is moving toward a demographic situation very similar to that prevailing throughout Western Europe.

This prediction is strengthened by an analysis of social class differentials. As in all other Western European countries, family planning in the Netherlands began among the urban upper and middle classes, and from there gradually spread to other social strata. Just as regional differences are now diminishing, class fertility rates also tend to converge again as modern contraceptive techniques come to be known and accepted on an ever-greater scale. We may see the whole trend as a typical example of modernization, and recognize such general aspects as rationalization, urbanization, and democratization. But although the direction of the trend fits a familiar pattern, we may still wonder at its pace. Granted that the idea of family planning is a part of a wider cultural complex, the question remains of why substantial segments of the Dutch population have been so slow in accepting this idea.

A specifically retarding factor has been, as Van Heek's studies have borne out, the influence of Roman Catholicism. In the middle of the nineteenth century the birth level of the Roman Catholics lay a little below the national average, probably because of the traditional restrictions on marriage. When, however, after 1880 the birth rate for the country as a whole began to drop, it remained high or even went up for most Roman Catholic districts. In the predominantly Roman Catholic provinces of North Brabant and Limburg, the decline did not set in until after 1910. By 1947 marital fertility in Roman Catholic families exceeded the national average by more than 25 per cent, a surplus that could not be attributed to differences in socioeconomic status.

A high fertility rate is in line with the official attitude of the Roman Catholic Church toward birth control. But this circumstance does not sufficiently explain the actual birth rate. In France and Belgium, which are nominally almost exclusively Roman Catholic countries, the birth rate is far lower than in the Netherlands, where Roman Catholics constitute less than 40 per cent of the population. Van Heek even found that Roman Catholic communities just across the border in Belgium and Germany usually have lower birth rates than the neighboring Dutch communities, in spite of a basically similar economic and social structure. The conclusion must be, then, that conditions in the Netherlands have been especially favorable to compliance with the official Church doctrine regarding birth control. The crucial factor appears to be the historic position of the Roman Catholics as a large minority with a strongly organized system of control. As Van Heek points out, the Dutch Roman Catholics have not shunned modern methods in defending their traditional policy. Internally they have protected their following from outside opinion by setting up an effective network of communications of their own covering every medium. Externally they have exerted strong pressure upon the national government to create throughout the country a climate unfavorable to birth control. Thus Roman Catholic initiative has introduced bills forbidding the public sale of contraceptives and has strongly supported a generous scheme of family subsidies with progressive rates for larger families.[5]

In recent years the birth rate of Dutch Roman Catholics has been declining. This may be interpreted as evidence that their insular position in Dutch society is waning. As yet, however, it is mainly the fertility of Roman Catholic marriages that raises the Dutch birth rate above the level of all other Western European countries.

Age

Age is the most conspicuous determinant of differential participation in social structure and culture. Being a continuous variable, however, biological age does not naturally give rise to clear-cut social categories. Its actual bearing upon social and cultural participation depends largely upon the definitions set by society. Thus, in the Netherlands the school age is legally defined as beginning at six, the voting age at twenty-one, the age for receiving a state pension at sixty-five, and so on. Even these administrative distinctions, however, have not brought about altogether unequivocal social age categories. The events signifying the transition from childhood to adulthood especially show a marked lack of "synchronization." [6] Scattered between the ages of fifteen and thirty lie the end of compulsory school education (at fifteen), the right to marry with parental consent (at sixteen for girls, eighteen for boys), the right to vote and majority before the law (both at twenty-one), the right to be elected for public office (at twenty-three and twenty-five, respectively, for municipal and national bodies), and as a last step toward adult independence, the right to marry without parental consent (at thirty).

As suggested by these examples, the age categories in Dutch society tend to have rather wide and overlapping margins. It is possible, nevertheless, to draw up a classification which, although imprecise in details, gives a valid general division. Thus, according to J. A. Ponsioen, we may distinguish five categories: *children,* up to the age of 14; *youth,* from 15 to 24; *younger adults,* from 25 to 39; *adults,* from 40 to 64; and the *aged,* 65 and older.[7] These successive age categories display some marked differences in social and cultural participation.

During childhood social participation is chiefly limited, first to family and neighborhood, and later to family, neighborhood, and school. There is no competition with adults for social position, and large parts of adult culture remain unknown. The period of youth considerably widens social and cultural perspectives. On the one hand, it marks the first initiation into adult culture, and on the other, it articulates the social class differentials in the acquisition of positions in the social structure. Most men start their occupational career during youth; the sooner they start working, however, the less likely they are to achieve a high socioeconomic status in later life. A prolonged school or university training, on the other hand, greatly increases the chances of upward social mobility. By the time youth ends, prospective career patterns are already clearly emerging. In fact, most working-class young men will have reached the ceiling of their occupational career before their contemporaries who are studying at the university have even made a start.

The category of youth is followed by that of the "younger adults," designated in the Dutch language by a special name: *jongeren*. This category finds its particular identity mainly in the upper and middle classes. The chief mark of the *jongere* appears to be that he is a full citizen who has completed his education and has achieved adult status as the head of a family of his own; yet in the organizational structure of Dutch society he still occupies a subordinate position. Culturally he is prepared for positions that are structurally not yet available. The situation resembles the conditions conducive to anomie as described by Robert Merton,[8] except for the positive time perspective involved: The *jongeren* look forward to attaining within a few years the positions held by their elders. During the waiting period, their attitude may be a mixture of critical detachment and ambitious deference toward the established powers. There are no official age limits defining the category of *jongeren*: as a consequence, a man of thirty-five or even thirty may occasionally attain a status that would normally be reserved for "full adults" only. In those cases, however, one will often find that the person concerned will "act older" than his real age. The important thing is that Dutch society has laid out a set of social positions and roles typically meant for *jongeren;* the fact that a few young men may quickly jump this stage while others stay within it well after they are forty does not alter its general significance.

Those in the age category 40 to 64 hold most of the leading positions in Dutch society. Thus the government and the two houses of parliament consist in an overwhelming majority of persons belonging to this category. People holding top positions in political or economic organizations often maintain them well over the age of 65.

In the lower brackets of the occupational hierarchy, however, the threat of dismissal and forced retirement may come earlier, and may be felt at any time after the age of 50. Here again socioeconomic status disturbs the synchronization of age categories.[9]

In general, the various age categories we have mentioned reflect the main turning points in occupational careers as important determinants of social and cultural participation. In this respect the age of 65 is becoming ever more crucial in marking the transition from regular work to retirement. Indeed, the two most significant social effects of the prolongation of life appear to be that the beginning of occupational careers for the young tends to be postponed, and the ending tends to be fixed at 65. Consequently, youth and the aged are becoming more clearly separate categories in society. Both are set apart from the adult categories in having structurally limited social opportunities and in having cultural facilities designed especially for them. The crucial difference is, of course, the time perspective; whereas youth is striving toward full adult status, the aged are in a process of disengagement.

The age categories in Dutch society are embedded in a changing social and cultural context, so that the individuals who come to populate a given age category in subsequent years will have had different life experiences. If these differences are sufficiently clear to mark off a category of contemporaries with a distinct historical identity, we may call this category a generation. Thus, in the history of modern Dutch literature, it is customary to distinguish the generations of 1880, 1910, 1920, and 1950 when referring to groups of writers who made their first appearance in print around these years with more or less explicit programs and whose work has continued to show traces of a common background. It is difficult, however, to assess how these manifestations of literary style are related to more widespread shifts in social and cultural orientation. No doubt the impact of modernization has thoroughly changed the way of life of successive generations. The process has not affected the whole population simultaneously, however; it reached the cities earlier than the countryside, the bourgeoisie earlier than the working classes, Holland earlier than Drente. This lack of synchronization makes unrealistic the classification of the entire population into generations. It seems reasonably likely that the sequence pointed out by David Riesman of tradition-directed, inner-directed, and other-directed social character pertains to the Netherlands as well as to the United States. But, as in America, the three stages do not necessarily denote distinct historical periods or generations, for they may very well coexist at the same time in various social milieux.[10]

Although it is impossible to retrace the long-range process of modernization in a succession of generations for Dutch society as a whole, there have been some specific events which do appear to have had such a general influence as to give rise to distinct generations. Thus it would seem to be important whether the period of youth coincided with the depression of the thirties, the Second World War, or the period of rising prosperity after 1950. The social and cultural prospects of these successive periods were markedly different; it seems likely that even today they still linger in people's attitudes toward society. This, however, is only a guess; the problem of generations in Dutch society remains largely to be investigated.[11]

Sex

As in other societies, modernization has brought about a shift in the Dutch sex ratio. For a long time there has been and there still is a birth surplus of boys of about 5 per cent. But since mortality also used to be higher among boys, the population as a whole has had a majority of women. In the twentieth century, however, owing to decreased childhood mortality, the surplus of men has tended to survive longer. Today the proportion of men to women in the total population is almost equal. But men and women are not evenly distributed as to age: under 35 men outnumber women, and over 35 there is a progressively higher ratio of women. This, combined with the tendency for women to marry at an earlier age than men, leads to a relatively high incidence of widows.

Apart from affecting the sex ratio, modernization has had a noticeable impact upon the positions and roles of men and women. Again, as in other societies, Dutch society has witnessed the "emancipation of women," with their social and cultural participation strengthened and discrimination between the sexes diminished. At least legally women have attained equal status with men since the formal barriers excluding them from the franchise, advanced education, and professional careers have been abolished. When in 1956 a woman was appointed as head of the Ministry of Social Work, one of the highest aims of feminism had apparently been reached. Yet the very fact that up till then no Dutch government had had a female minister indicates the continuing disparity between male and female participation in matters of a national scope. Not merely in politics, but in all main institutional areas, women share the fate of the *jongeren:* They are fully entitled to achieve prominence, and usually there are a few successful individuals who have managed to demonstrate this, but still their category as a whole remains heavily underrepresented in the leading positions of society. Thus, to give but one more example, among the chief executives of large companies, less than one-half of one per cent are women.[12]

The underlying causes of this disparity are probably to be found in the distribution of masculine and feminine roles within the family. According to law, the man still is the "head" of the family; he is supposed to maintain its material well-being by his earnings. For the married woman, the prevailing norm is that her task lies within the family household; she is not primarily expected to earn money, but to spend it in a way that is beneficial to the family. Thus, according to the mutually ascribed responsibilities, the dominant masculine role is occupational; the dominant feminine role, domestic.

At an early age children are prepared for this role differentiation, both by the examples of their parents and by the approval or disapproval given to their own behavior. Formal education, except for some vocational training schools, does not officially discriminate between the sexes. Curriculums are basically the same, and attendance is usually mixed. Still, at the secondary school level the ways of boys and girls tend to part; over the age of 14 almost 40 per cent more boys than girls are receiving full-time instruction.

Women constitute about one quarter of the total labor force. Curiously, the same proportion was reported in the census of 1889. But although the total share of gainfully employed women has hardly changed, the social composition of this category is substantially different today. In 1889 almost all female workers were manual workers, many of whom were married and had children. Today they are found in all sorts of occupations, and only a minority are married. The right to work, gained by the feminist movement, has been primarily a benefit to middle-class women; at the same time democratization has brought a considerable relief from the necessity to work to the women of the lower classes.

As a rule, wages for women are considerably lower than

wages for men. The prestige attached to female occupations also tends to be less. Discrimination is particularly effective with regard to married women; as a result, the Netherlands has a strikingly small number of married women with jobs (see Table 3). All this seems to be re-

TABLE 3

Percentages of Women in the Labor Force of Various Countries, 1960

	All Women	Married Women Only
Netherlands	28.5	3.0
United States	48.0	26.0
Germany	60.0	32.0
England	52.0	27.0
France	53.0	27.0

SOURCE: Nederlands Normalisatie Instituut, quoted in *De Onderneming,* October 31, 1961.

lated to the retarded impact of modernization. Apparently the middle-class norm allotting woman her main task inside her home still prevails. This norm is sustained by the prevailing system of taxation, which adds the income of married women to that of their husbands so that, with the progressively rated tax scales, they are more heavily burdened.

The social category of women has not produced any organization commensurate with its numbers. To the majority of women, family affiliations outweigh sex solidarity. This attitude is indicated by the small number of preferential votes received by female candidates at elections; it is revealed in another way in the avowedly apolitical and family-oriented contents of the highly popular magazines for women. Despite the emancipation movement, Dutch society remains in its organizational structure predominantly controlled by men.

Creed

The Dutch population has a varied religious composition, and religious distinctions permeate many areas of social life. As pointed out in Chapter II, both the coexistence of several religious denominations and the particular significance attached to them reach back to the events of the Reformation in the sixteenth century. In that crucial period only a part of the population went over to the Protestant faith. The southern provinces remained wholly Roman Catholic, while in the northern regions quite a few enclaves of Catholicism survived. Moreover, from the very beginning Protestantism itself was divided into two mainstreams: doctrinaire Calvinism on the one hand and a more liberal and tolerant tradition on the other. Finally, the process of secularization in the late nineteenth and twentieth centuries has produced a category of people not affiliated with any church.

The distinctions between these four categories do not end with formal church membership; they are carried over into many other spheres. The ensuing situation is so intrinsically Dutch that only the Dutch language has evolved an appropriate vocabulary to deal with it. We have already mentioned the word *verzuiling* or "pillarization," meaning the tendency for religious blocs or "pillars" to penetrate into institutions of a nonreligious character. Several other terms have developed in the same context. Thus *volksdeel,* or "part of the population" is used to encompass the people belonging to any particular bloc; *levensbeschouwelijk,* the adjective form pertaining to *levensbeschouwing* or "view of life" serves to indicate the ideational differences between the blocs, including the nonreligious bloc; similarly, *buitenkerkelijke* is meant as an inoffensive cognate for those who are literally "outside the church" (they are also known as *onkerkelijken* or the "unchurchly"); *andersdenkende,* meaning "thinking in another way," is the common neutral noun to designate those who are in different blocs from one's own. All these words are in ordinary usage; the phenomenon of "pillarization" and all there is to it belongs to the most obvious and generally recognized properties of the Dutch social and cultural scene.

Religious creed, then, is a paramount criterion for categorizing the Dutch population. Unfortunately, the actual numbers of adherents to the major creeds are hard to give precisely. Religion is a far more difficult variable to grasp than either age or sex. The only data we have are the census figures, which record alleged church membership without any further specification of the meaning of religion in the respondent's personal or social life. Still, as

TABLE 4

Registered Church Affiliation in Percentages of the Dutch Population, 1849–1960

| | Religious Affiliation | | | | |
Year	Roman Catholic	Dutch Reformed	Gerefor- meerd	Others	None
1849	38.1	54.6	1.3	6.0	0.0
1859	37.1	54.9	2.0	5.9	0.1
1869	36.5	54.7	3.0	5.7	0.1
1879	35.9	54.5	3.5	5.8	0.3
1889	35.4	48.6	8.2	6.3	1.5
1899	35.1	48.4	8.2	6.0	2.3
1909	35.0	44.2	9.4	6.4	5.0
1920	35.6	41.2	9.1	6.3	7.8
1930	36.4	34.5	9.3	5.4	14.4
1947	38.5	31.1	9.7	3.7	17.1
1960	40.4	28.3	9.3	3.6	18.4

SOURCE: Netherlands Central Bureau of Statistics, *Census Results.*

58292

shown in Table 4, the available data give a valuable insight into the main trends of the last century.

First of all, we see the arrested growth in the numbers of Roman Catholics during the nineteenth century and the headway they have made in the past decades. The table does not convey the fact, however, that the recent advance does not quite keep pace with the high birth level in this category. The cause of this discrepancy apparently lies in apostasy among adults. As a result, the mean age of the Roman Catholic population is strikingly young.

The reverse situation applies to those of the Dutch Reformed creed, who constitute an aging category. Their decline since 1850, both in relative size and importance, has been remarkable. Even among the dwindled numbers of today there are many purely nominal members. The losses have been in two directions; those who left were either orthodox Calvinists withdrawing to join more fundamentalist churches or liberals and latitudinarians passing over into the category of the "unchurchly."

The third category in Table 4, the *Gereformeerden*, have maintained the gains made in the second half of the nineteenth century. They belong to various churches, some organized nationally, others of only a regional or local stature, each of which claims to continue the true tradition of the Reformation in the Netherlands. It is, again, impossible to give a literal translation of the contrast between *Hervormd* as in *Nederlands Hervormd* and *Gereformeerd,* both terms meaning "reformed." The actual distinction is quite important, however. We shall express it by consistently translating *Nederlands Hervormd* into Dutch Reformed and by continuing to refer to the various seceded churches of staunchly Calvinist imprint as *Gereformeerd*.

The category "Others" comprises, as the name suggests, a heterogeneous congeries of small churches, ranging from liberal to fundamentalist. The decrease of the past decades has been mainly due to losses on the liberal side. Also included in this category are the adherents of the Jewish faith, who were almost annihilated during the Second World War; between the censuses of 1930 and 1947 their numbers dropped from 112,000 to 14,000.

The category of the "unchurchly" has been increasing steadily. In official statistics the term "unchurchly" has been preferred to "irreligious" in order to include those who profess to being religious without being affiliated to any particular church. The present percentage of the registered "unchurchly" is very high in comparison with most other Western societies. This does not, however, necessarily point toward greater indifference to church ties than elsewhere; rather, the high incidence of respondents claiming to be "unchurchly" appears to reflect an outspoken awareness of "where one stands" in religious matters.[13]

The five statistical categories based upon alleged church membership do not quite correspond to the relevant sociological categories we mentioned in the first paragraph of this section. Since they include both fundamentalists and latitudinarians, the two categories of "Dutch Reformed" and "Others" do not have an unequivocal social and cultural significance. The Roman Catholics and the *Gereformeerden,* on the other hand, do constitute rather homogeneous and close-knit religious groupings with a marked identity of their own. The Roman Catholic Church in the Netherlands forms part of a great international organization. Whereas in all Dutch Protestant churches the congregation either directly or indirectly elects its own minister, Roman Catholic priests are appointed by central authority. There are other distinctive characteristics, both in dogma and ritual and in social structure. Sanctification, mass, confession, special holidays, monastic orders, celi-

bacy of priests, clerical dress, processions—by such features Roman Catholicism clearly stands out in Dutch society. A Roman Catholic home can be recognized by the
presence of a crucifix, as can a Roman Catholic married
man or woman because, unlike the Dutch Protestants,
they wear their wedding ring on the left hand.

The typically distinguishing traits of the *Gereformeerden,* in contrast, are an emphatic devotion to Scripture
and a rigorous striving to practice God's word in daily life.
Their theology puts a heavy accent upon sin and reproba-
tion; from this they derive a stern morality dictating strict
obedience to biblical demands such as Sunday observance.
The same tendencies prevail among a large minority in
the Dutch Reformed Church. Altogether the *Gereformeerden* in their scriptural strictness often show a tendency toward sectarianism; thus, in Rijsen, Overijsel, a
town of 15,000 inhabitants, no less than seven different
variants of Reformed churches coexist. Awareness of such
tendencies finds expression in the sally: "One Dutchman
a theologian, two Dutchmen a church, three Dutchmen a
schism." [14]

Besides implying distinct theological and ethical commitments, church affiliation is also related to several other
social characteristics. Most notable in this respect are,
again, the Roman Catholics. On the average they are
younger than any other religious category; they have a
higher birth rate; they form solid numerical majorities of
about 90 per cent in the provinces of North Brabant and
Limburg. Their position in the educational and occupational structure still reflects the subdued part they used to
play in Dutch society. Although in recent decades they
have been catching up rapidly, they are still lagging in
their relative share of secondary school and university students as well as of professional persons and civil servants.
Likewise, in recent intelligence surveys they have tended

to score lower than any other religious category.[15] In striking contrast stand some of the minor Protestant churches of liberal inclination (categorized under "Others" in Table 4) which, considering their small numbers, display an intensive participation in the higher educational and occupational levels.

In its overall effect upon social and cultural participation, religion is of the utmost importance. To begin with, it strongly determines the choice among the three prevailing types of school: public, Protestant, or Roman Catholic. Thus at the age of six the population is already divided into three separate blocs, who spend a great deal of their time in different kinds of environments and receive different kinds of instruction in such subjects as religion and history. Since the system of formal education is almost wholly "pillarized," one may receive the most extensive university education without ever leaving one's own bloc. The divisions thus brought about in youth persist in adulthood: Political parties, trade unions, mass media, leisure associations, health and welfare organizations all follow the principle of "pillarization"; in almost any field each bloc has its own separate apparatus. To complicate matters, the religiously moderate or indifferent bloc is sometimes split up into conservative and socialist segments, both operating as full-fledged "pillars." We shall discuss this phenomenon at greater length in the chapter on national integration.

Religious differentiation also leaves its marks upon social life in the private sphere. In a community study in the bulb-growing town of Sassenheim, South Holland, a social distance scale revealed that 81.9 per cent of the people objected to marriage between partners of different creeds, 40.6 per cent to their being friends, and 11.4 per cent to their working together. Discrimination was expressed most strongly by Roman Catholics, successively followed by *Gereformeerden,* Dutch Reformed, and "un-churchly." No such objections were made by only 15.8 per cent of the respondents, most of whom belonged to either the "unchurchly" or the Dutch Reformed. It should be added that these results were obtained in 1952 in a predominantly rural community; in a city, attitudes probably would have been less extreme. Still, they do give an impression of the extent to which religious distinctions guide social relationships.[16]

This impression is confirmed by the low incidence of intercreed marriages, for which national figures are available. In Dutch this phenomenon is known as "mixed marriage," a telling name. In 1957, out of every 100 marrying Roman Catholics, an average of 9.2 concluded a mixed marriage; this percentage was 23.1 for the *Gereformeerden,* 24.6 for the Dutch Reformed, 31.9 for the "unchurchly," and 58.7 for the other denominations. The peculiarity of the Dutch situation is revealed by comparison with the figures for Roman Catholics marrying outside their religion in Germany and Switzerland, which in the same year were 24.7 and 22.6 per cent, respectively. Since the categories differ in size, the chances for a mixed marriage are unequal; yet even when this probability factor is taken into account, the Dutch figure remains remarkably low.[17]

Given the relative insularity of religious communities, it is small wonder that religious ties tend to follow traditional lines. In the Sassenheim study more than 80 per cent of the respondents appeared to belong to the same church as their fathers' fathers.[18] Even the process of secularization, which has caused a momentous shift in the denominational composition of the population at large, has made its impact gradually rather than abruptly. In some areas indifference to religion has already been a matter of long-standing tradition. As the available evidence sug-

gests, apostasy seldom occurs suddenly; a definitive break
with the church usually is the outcome of a drifting-away
tendency extending over two or three generations.[19] As in
other countries, intellectuals, professionals, and industrial
workers are most prone to "backsliding." The most notable
aspect of secularization in Dutch society remains its manifestation in official statistics. In several municipalities, including the city of Amsterdam, as well as in some rural
districts in the northern provinces, almost half or more of
the population is registered as "unchurchly."

Residence

The small territory of the Netherlands comprises a great
variety of regions. One usually needs to travel but a short
distance in order to come across localities of a markedly
divergent character. Thus, within a range of fifteen miles
from the city of Amsterdam, we find the fashionable com-
muter area of Het Gooi, the bleak *polder* landscape of
Haarlemmermeer, the busy industrial Zaan district, and
the quaint old fishing towns of Marken and Volendam,
famous as tourist attractions. Any other point of departure
might lead to a similar variety of settlements displaying, in
spite of close proximity, conspicuous differences in scen-
ery, layout of roads and streets, architecture, and economy. In addition, a trained ear would notice a proliferation of local and regional tongues. Even the physical type
of men is not quite the same in different parts of the
country; in the northern provinces the prevalence of
blond and blue- or grey-eyed persons is greater than in the
South; military recruits from Friesland measure almost 2
inches taller than those from Limburg. These differences,
of course, obtain for provincial averages only; it is quite
impossible to infer someone's local origins from his physical appearance. The various stocks out of which the

Dutch people is composed have blended beyond recognition.

In general, regional variety reflects the survival of historic influences. In the past geographic isolation fostered the development of regional and local traditions. People growing up in a certain area would naturally take over its particular customs. Today, however, with increasing national integration, spatial boundaries exert a far less binding influence. One of the most important aspects of modernization is that as industrialization and specialization release men from their immediate dependence upon the soil, the traditional local ties lose much of their significance and are increasingly replaced by social ties extending over ever larger geographical distances. Consequently, residence recedes as a determinant of social and cultural participation.

It has not yet lost all significance, however. On the basis of residence we may still discern at least three major dividing lines splitting the Dutch population into distinct social categories: the "West-rest," the North-South, and the urban-rural divisions. The first of these, the "West-rest" dichotomy, proceeds from the historic predominance of Holland which, in spite of countervailing influences, is still tangible today. Although covering but slightly over one-fifth of the total land area, the three western provinces of North and South Holland and Utrecht contain almost half of the Dutch population. The economic, social, and cultural facilities offered by these provinces continue to attract a steady influx of migrants from other parts of the country. Here in the western provinces, industrialization and urbanization have advanced a great deal further; consequently, opportunities for industrial and administrative employment are more varied, and the supply of goods and services is considerably higher. Further indices of western advantages are, for example, a denser distribution of households having electricity, water, gas, and telephone; an appreciably higher expenditure per person on concerts and theater; a more widespread secondary school attendance; a higher proportion of university graduates; and a mean I.Q. above the national average.[20]

An additional exponent of the continuing prevalence of Holland is the Dutch national standard language, which is modeled after the idiom spoken by the Holland, and especially the Amsterdam, elites. To ordinary people in many parts of the country, this idiom is still felt to be strange. Yet it is taught at all schools, and mastery of it is almost a prerequisite for social success above a barely local level. Thus standards of behavior originally conceived in Holland now pertain to Dutch society at large; the "West" is serving as an example to the "rest."

If we take speech as a criterion, the region most overtly resistant to the overall cultural dominance of Holland appears to be the South. Leading representatives from the provinces of North Brabant and Limburg usually speak the national standard language with an accent clearly revealing their southern origin. Thus the second main regional division, North-South, makes itself heard. The beginnings of this division, again, lie in the late sixteenth and early seventeenth centuries, when the territories of North Brabant and Limburg were reconquered from the Spanish and subjugated to direct rule from The Hague. The ensuing regime, which lasted for two centuries, left these provinces politically powerless, and through a system of unduly heavy taxation, greatly hampered their economic development. It did not force the population to embrace Protestantism, however, and as a result the whole region has remained almost solidly Roman Catholic up to the present day. Along with Roman Catholicism, the two centuries of virtual isolation have left an imprint upon the whole way of life. In a recent nationwide study of norms and values, the Dutch sociologist I. Gadourek concludes that the South and the North are "the two main subcultures in the Netherlands":

> Over against the more optimistic, vivacious Roman Catholic or Southern pattern, emphasizing sexual morality, stands the more sombre and sober, and more matter-of-fact Protestant-Calvinistic or Northern way of life, disapproving most of lies and theft.[21]

Both the "West-rest" and the North-South divisions are cut across by the urban-rural dichotomy. As pointed out earlier, the latter distinction is losing its sharpness now that urban influences are spreading into even the remotest rural districts. Today the typical contrast is even hard to define. Until the end of the eighteenth century cities used to be clearly distinguished by their special rights and, in most cases, by being walled in by fortifications. Today's cities have neither a distinct legal status nor a particular military importance; instead, they are recognized by such demographic characteristics as the size, the density, and the occupational structure of their populations. All of these criteria are continuous variables; in applying the words "city" and "urban," therefore, we have to set some arbitrary limits.

In the process of urbanization, the rural areas tend to become more or less a residual category—that part of the country that is not yet wholly urbanized. Many parts of the countryside have already virtually been converted into "ex-urbanite" colonies used for residential or recreational purposes. Only 10 per cent of the population today is working in agrarian occupations, and it has been estimated that a further decline toward 5 per cent lies ahead. Numerous small villages have been hit hard by the "rural exodus" set in motion where attempts at providing new employment in trade or industry have failed. Moreover, apart from the economic challenge, the countryside as a whole is facing the general problem of "viability" caused by the relatively meager supply of nearby social and cultural facilities. This difficulty appears to be most pressing in the more prosperous and progressive areas, where at the same time physical distances between facilities are apt to be the greatest and the demand for modern urban services most deeply felt.

The causes of this tension, as A. K. Constandse suggests, lie in the fact that people who are "mentally urban" find themselves living in a "physically rural" environment.[22] In the Netherlands the city population has always enjoyed social and cultural advantages over the rural population. What is new today is the extent to which the rural population is applying urban standards to its own way of life. A general norm of comfortable and convenient living is gaining acceptance among city and rural folk alike; at the moment, however, it is causing more frustration among the latter.

In some respects the rural areas as a whole are still lagging in modernization. Thus, to mention two typical examples, they have a lower secondary school attendance and a higher birth rate. Since some rural districts are particularly advanced in these very same respects, however, it does not seem unlikely that in the long run these differences will diminish and perhaps disappear altogether. On the whole, as territorial ties make way for more extensive social ties of a functionally specific nature, the urban-rural dichotomy will become less important, as will the regional locus of residence.

Socioeconomic Status

One of the most important criteria making for distinct social categories is socioeconomic status. Its pertinence regarding differential participation hardly needs comment; already by definition the concept refers to a specific position in society implying a specific cultural orientation. For two reasons, however, socioeconomic status is more difficult to pinpoint than any of the criteria discussed so far. In the first place, it is not officially recognized as such and can therefore only indirectly be inferred from other data, and second, instead of being a well-defined, homogeneous characteristic, it is made up of various components whose internal relationships are not always clear.

In the nineteenth century few ambiguities attached to social status. Society consisted of some generally acknowledged *standen* or "estates," each of which had a particular style of life. Almost always it was clearly evident whether a person belonged to the *stand* of burghers or workmen or farmers; more often than not, his specific station within his *stand* could be equally well ascertained. Forms of address varied according to social rank: the title of *mijnheer*, sometimes used by English novelists to indicate any Dutch character, was strictly reserved for burghers, the common people being called by either their surname or, for the lowest in rank, by their first name.

The prevailing social and cultural differences corresponded unequivocally to the economic division of society into the rich and the poor. A Marxian observer would have found ample evidence in the nineteenth-century Netherlands for the thesis that society was moving in the direction of an increasing estrangement between the two classes, the capitalist and the proletarian. Here as elsewhere, however, actual developments in the twentieth century have taken quite another turn. Instead of deteriorating, the conditions of the working class have greatly improved. Pauperism has all but disappeared; some former bourgeois privileges such as political franchise or holidays from work have been extended to the entire population, while others, like the substitute system that enabled rich men to buy immunity from military service, have been altogether abolished.

Today *stand* and class are unpopular subjects in the Netherlands. In contrast to *verzuiling*, social stratification is seldom made the topic of public discussion. Occasionally a case of social discrimination by landlords or housing cooperatives makes the news. These incidents invariably arouse a widespread indignation that suggests that such behavior is not tolerated in the democratic society of the Netherlands. The common practice of market research agencies of classifying respondents as "A/B: the well-to-do; C: the middle group; D1: the less well-to-do; D2: the least well-to-do" [23] neatly expresses the attitude prevailing in Dutch society today; that is, an inevitable awareness of socioeconomic differences hampered by a reluctance to mention them outright. Even sociologists have tended to shun the subject—they have produced many valuable statistical reports bearing on various aspects of socioeconomic status, but so far no attempt has been made at a comprehensive analysis of social classes in contemporary Dutch society.

Our discussion of socioeconomic status will draw only upon published statistical records, taking occupation as the point of departure. In a direct sense, of course, classification by occupation includes only the 40 per cent of the population who are actively engaged in earning a living. Indirectly, however, occupation is pertinent to the whole population, since the occupation of the head of a household reflects upon the income, style of life, social prestige, and social contacts of all members of the family. On this ground, occupation may be regarded as an important indicator of socioeconomic status.

There are several ways of classifying occupations into relevant social categories. To begin with, *economic func-*

tion may be taken as a criterion.[24] Thus in 1960, 15 per cent of the total working population was engaged in the primary sector (mainly agriculture, fishing, and mining), 47 per cent in the secondary sector (mainly industry and crafts), and 38 per cent in the tertiary sector (mainly administration and services). The most striking long-term developments in the distribution of economic functions have been, as already mentioned, the decline of agriculture, accompanied by the expansion of industry and the even greater growth of administrative and service occupations. Within the latter category a countermovement has also taken place: the gradual diminution of household servants from 25 per cent of the labor force in 1850 to a bare 2.8 per cent in 1960. Just as the decline of agriculture signifies a diminishing dependency upon the soil, so does the shrinkage of menial household occupations point toward a release from extreme personal subservience. Thus both shifts in economic function express the rise of more complicated and extended social interdependencies.

A second important differentiating factor in relation to occupation is *size of income*. This, too, must be seen in a historical perspective against the background of a long-term rise in national productivity and prosperity. For the population at large, real income per capita has increased at least two and a half times since 1860. To this must be added a wholesale rise in public services. As a result, inequalities in income have become less pronounced, although they have by no means disappeared. Official statistics refer to taxable income only, without taking into account such hidden revenues as capital gains, benefits in kind, and concealed wages. In spite of these shortcomings, however, the available data give a fair overall impression of the range of incomes. Roughly speaking, of the total personal income received in the Netherlands, one-third accrues to 10 per cent of the population, another third to

25 per cent, and the remaining third to 65 per cent. The relative share of the upper 10 per cent is slightly larger than in comparable countries like Sweden or England; on the whole, however, Dutch income distribution follows the pattern found in most Western European countries.[25]

Whereas the continuous range of incomes ranked according to size does not disclose any clear-cut social categories, a significant dichotomy emerges when we consider *source of income*. In 1960, 70 per cent of all taxpayers received salaries, wages, or pensions, and 30 per cent lived on the proceeds of their own business or property. There is a slow but steady trend for the number of those who are employed to increase relative to the number of those who are economically independent. In addition, the latter find themselves more and more subjected to various sorts of central control, exercised either by the government or by self-imposed coordinating agencies. Still, in spite of this tendency away from altogether free enterprise, the two categories maintain markedly distinct positions in the nation's economy, with important social and cultural concomitants. Thus, the independent have an average income more than twice as large as the employed. Independent businessmen are more likely to feel taxation as a heavy burden and to object to what they consider state curtailment of private initiative. In comparison with salaried employees in the same income brackets, they have less time to spend on leisure, and they therefore engage less frequently in recreational pursuits outside their occupations; moreover, they are inclined to attach less value to formal education, both for themselves and for their children.[26]

Within the category of the employed, we may distinguish the *kind of work* as manual and nonmanual or "blue" and "white" collar occupations. In line with the expansion of tertiary economic functions, the white collar category enlarged its share of the number of the employed from 37 per cent in 1947 to 42 per cent in 1959.[27] The two categories differ, first of all, in their actual employment situations: As a rule the manual worker works longer hours; he receives his wage (as distinguished from "salary") per week; in case of illness he gets no payment for the first one or two days; he may give or receive notice of only a few weeks' time; he is more intensively supervised; he often receives piece rates for his actual output; he does not share in bonus dividends. These "formal" distinctions are upheld in the majority of Dutch firms; together they

> reflect underlying attitudes: the piece remunerations express that the worker is being paid for a quantity of work, and not for a function; the first unpaid days in case of illness indicate that he is not quite trusted in the event of a short absence; the weekly payment of his wages voices doubt as to his and his wife's capacity to spend the income well; the shorter term of notice testifies to his ready replaceability and the small value at which his loyalty to the firm is estimated.[28]

Thus manual and nonmanual labor are given different treatment. As J. A. A. van Doorn shows, these discriminatory regulations tend to be mitigated as specialization and mechanization put many office tasks on a par with factory work. Still, important differences remain. Most companies provide better avenues for individual advancement to their white collar employees, either through chances of promotion or through seniority rights; as a result, their company loyalty tends to be stronger and their class solidarity weaker. White collar salaries range up to quite high extremes; singularly successful employees may even reach the top of the corporate hierarchy and pass over into the category of chief executives, the highest paid occupational category in the Netherlands.[29]

The differences between manual and nonmanual workers are not confined to the sphere of work. In general, social interaction between the two categories tends to be limited, and if facilitated by residence, it is not always appreciated. Cultural participation is also unequal; although there is no sharp dividing point, manual workers by and large tend to take less interest in such aspects of national culture as higher learning, classical music, and literature. This lack of interest may be explained largely on the grounds of relatively poor schooling, an intervening variable of great importance in perpetuating the existing social and cultural disparities.[30]

In many respects the distinction between manual and nonmanual workers can be interpreted as a matter of *social prestige*. Thanks to Van Heek and his associates, the social prestige attached to various occupations is one of the most thoroughly investigated aspects of Dutch society.[31] In 1953 a national sample of the population was asked to rank 57 occupations according to social esteem. A rank-order was found to exist, valid for the nation as a whole, and tallying in its general tendency with the rank-orders revealed in earlier local studies. The 57 separate items were then contracted into 6 broad categories designated as social layers or strata. Through various means of interpolation, data obtained in other investigations were included in this sixfold division, so that the following scale including virtually all occupations could be constructed:

STRATUM 1. *Mainly professionals and university graduates, directors of large companies, secondary school teachers, high-ranking civil servants—totaling 3 per cent of the population.*

STRATUM II. *Mainly high-ranking managerial and executive employees and civil servants, directors of small companies, large-scale farmers, trained technicians—totaling 8 per cent of the population.*

STRATUM III. *Mainly medium- and large-scale shopkeepers and artisans, medium farmers, medium-ranking white collar employees and civil servants—totaling 20 per cent of the population.*

STRATUM IV. *Mainly skilled manual workers, small shopkeepers and artisans, small farmers, low-ranking white collar employees and civil servants—totaling 34 per cent of the population.*

STRATUM V. *Mainly semi-skilled manual workers, lowest-ranking officials—totaling 27 per cent of the population.*

STRATUM VI. *Mainly unskilled manual workers—totaling 8 per cent of the population.*

At first sight the rank-order of occupational prestige is seen to be linked to size of income; even more pertinent, however, appears to be the relation to formal education. In the original list of 57 occupations, "university professor" ranked highest of all, followed by "physician," "mayor of a large city," "judge," "engineer," "notary public," "lawyer," "dentist," and in ninth place, just above "veterinarian," "director of a large company." The bias placing education above, for instance, income or power, is evident, and it is hardly surprising that upon closer analysis, high occupational prestige was found to correlate positively with length of school education. Other correlates proved to be a small-sized family of origin, living in a large city, living in one of the western provinces, and finally, religious affiliation, in the following order: (1) "Others," (2) *Gereformeerden,* (3) Dutch Reformed, (4) Unchurchly,

(5) Roman Catholic. The religious factor, in turn, corre-
lated with length of school education and family size.

A measure of the social impact of occupational prestige
is the degree of endogamy within each of the prestige
categories. Comparing the socioeconomic background of
their fathers and their fathers-in-law, it was found that 38
per cent of all bridegrooms had married into the same
category, 41 per cent into an immediately adjoining category, and the remaining 21 per cent into a category two or
three layers away from their own. Interestingly, there is a
slight but unmistakable tendency for men to marry upward and for women to marry downward—a tendency
which must necessarily result in a somewhat higher ratio
of unmarried women in the upper strata and unmarried
men in the lower strata.

The studies of occupational prestige have also supplied
valuable information regarding *occupational mobility*. In
the period from 1919 to 1954, the total Dutch labor force
has increased by over 50 per cent. This increase has not
been the same in all strata, however; it ranged from 152
per cent in stratum I to only 19 per cent in stratum VI. In
other words, the highly qualified occupations have expanded a great deal, while the unskilled and menial occupations have lagged behind in the general increment. This
corroborates our observations with regard to the shift in
economic functions.

Of all persons engaged in an occupation during the
whole period from 1919 through 1954, 30 per cent have
in the course of their careers ascended on the occupational
prestige scale, and 9 per cent have descended. For this
entire group, upward mobility was at its peak when they
were between the ages of 25 to 30; it then waned in the
next ten years, and became virtually absent or nullified by
retrogressions after 40. In comparison with their fathers,
37 per cent of the men in this group had moved upward,

and 23 per cent downward. Unfortunately, the occupational prestige scale used in the Dutch investigation and those used in other European surveys are not identical. Exact international comparisons of mobility are therefore ruled out, but in general, the situation in the Netherlands does not seem to differ much from that elsewhere in Western Europe.[32] The overall appraisal of occupational mobility depends very much upon choice of words: we may refer to it equally well as "widespread" or as "limited." In any case, spectacular rises or descents seldom occur. The total situation is one of relative calm; there is a general upgrading movement in which the whole population is sharing, some with greater success than others. The key to social ascent is, increasingly, education.

As pointed out above, the whole issue of social stratification in Dutch society has so far received only limited sociological attention. The crucial problem of the interrelationships between wealth, prestige, and power still awaits investigation. Only one social class in the Netherlands has so far been empirically studied and reported, and that is the lowest class—the unskilled laborers and the inhabitants of the urban slums. For the rest, little is known about the actual dynamics of stratification, and least of all is known about the elites.[33] One may be tempted to ascribe this lack of information to the persisting dominance of the leading *burgerij* or bourgeoisie, for whom discretion has always been part and parcel of its self-assured dignity and authority; the modern university graduates, ascended from lower levels of society, have generally tended without questioning to adopt this paternalistic attitude, known in Dutch as *regentenmentaliteit* or "regent mentality." But this is as yet no more than an impression; one can only hope for future research in this area.

{IV}

National Integration

The Netherlands, although small, is a fully developed national society, possessing all of nationhood's appropriate institutions and organizations: governmental, political, educational, and so forth. It would be impossible to describe this national network here in all its ramifications; what we shall do is to survey some of the areas where national unity is most manifest: the state, politics, the school system, the economy, and organized leisure. Our purpose will be to point out how in these respective areas the various social segments we discussed in the preceding chapter are coordinated within one national system.

In this context it will be helpful to bear in mind the historical perspective outlined in Chapter II. The national unity of Dutch society dates back to the late sixteenth century; it has subsisted with remarkable stability since. For a long time, however, a rather great social and cultural distance prevailed between the national center, located in the cities in the western provinces, and the rest of the society. The few existing national organizations (notably the States-General of the Republic and the Dutch Reformed Church) were controlled by relatively small burgher elites. The majority of the people lived within the confines of their communities and regions, peripheral to the national center.

Modernization has drawn Dutch society ever closer within the orbit of the world economy and world politics, and has opened up traditionally closed communities. The growing importance of transnational relationships has brought about a profusion of national organizations mediating between the Dutch and the rest of the world. Since the middle of the nineteenth century, the national framework has steadily expanded and penetrated more deeply into previously isolated segments of society—a process still in full swing today. Once started, this trend receives impulses from both ends, as it were: Already established national organizations grow bigger and stronger while, at the same time, formerly unorganized sections of the population enter the national scene on their own accord, availing themselves of national association as a means of improving their position in society.

Partly owing to its relatively late start, modernization has proceeded in the Netherlands in a gradual way, without revolutionary shocks. As a result, today's national social structure and culture show a marked continuity with the patterns set in previous centuries. Thus, the western part of the country still houses the main national political, economic, and cultural centers. Similarly, the way of life of the burgher aristocracy continues to carry great prestige, even though the actual power of the old elites has diminished. Indeed, as pointed out in Chapter II, bourgeois civility is still a cultural prerequisite for social success in any national organization. Finally, religious diversity has remained a pervasive determinant of social and cultural distinctions, giving rise to the curious phenomenon of "bloc" formation known as *verzuiling*. The bloc of liberal burghers, dominant in the middle of the nineteenth century, has been joined by rival blocs of Orthodox Calvinists, Roman Catholics, and socialists as closely organized competitors for power in almost every sphere of social life. This fourfold division—which sometimes appears as threefold or fivefold because of *ad hoc* alliances or minor secessions—influences the national integration of Dutch society in a crucial way.

The State

The state is the most effective of all organizations fostering national unity. It can be so effective because it possesses the monopoly of organized physical force and therefore of coercion. Commanding the ultimate sanction of persecution and imprisonment, the state can compel its subjects to perform civil duties such as paying taxes and obeying the law. In return, the state may provide services ranging from the maintenance of peace and order to very specialized economic, social, and cultural facilities for various groups. Many of these services, again, have an obligatory character; thus, for example, people are required by law to send their children to school and to join social insurance schemes. As the body of legislation grows, the net effect of the increasing role of governmental functions is to draw the entire population closer within one nationally organized system of social control and, concurrently, to diffuse uniform cultural standards of "civility."

The Dutch state is a unitary state. This implies that in the Netherlands the central national government possesses a more exclusive authority than in the federal structures of the United States or Switzerland. Today's unitary state differs greatly from the old Dutch Republic, which was a rather loose confederation of seven provinces, each of which remained nominally sovereign and preserved a great deal of practical autonomy in arranging its own jurisdiction, taxation, and even coinage. After the collapse of the Republic in 1795, followed by a period of French domination, the Dutch state received its present shape as a monarchy at the Congress of Vienna in 1815. There are today eleven provinces and over 900 municipalities, which are viewed as "lower organs" and are subject to the same uniform national arrangements. Some allowance is still made for decentralized authority; but since all major taxes are collected by the national government, the provinces and municipalities have to rely for most of their finances upon the central treasury in The Hague, which puts a severe restriction upon their actual autonomy. In every important field of state activity, the same centrally issued regulations obtain; this holds true for the enforcement of law, the collection of revenue, military recruitment, the organization and financing of schools, and the whole array of social and economic services and controls.

The unity of the Dutch state is symbolized in the monarchy. When in 1813 the first king of the House of Orange acceded to the throne, he was given ample personal power. A thorough revision of the Constitution in 1848 and the successive acceptance of restrictive customary rules have reduced this power to a minimum. Official procedures and documents still pay ceremonial tribute to the Crown; thus every new government is duly appointed by the ruling king or queen, and all acts of parliament are proclaimed by royal consent. Actually the functions of the monarch are mainly symbolic, the king representing both the unity of the people—he is supposed to be elevated above party struggles—and the continuity of authority:

the hereditary monarchy survives the vicissitudes of elections and political crises.

A basic clause put into the Constitution in 1848 states that "the King is inviolable and the ministers are responsible." This means that actual governmental policies are carried out by a board of ministers (the "cabinet"), who have to account for their actions to parliament. The members of parliament are elected at regular four-year intervals by all adult Dutch citizens; together they thus represent the people. In case of a conflict between the cabinet and parliament, the cabinet must either resign or call a new election. If in the latter case the newly formed parliament also refuses its consent, the cabinet has no choice but to resign. These arrangements plainly put the Dutch state upon a democratic basis; the government always owes responsibility to the representatives chosen by the people.

The parliamentary system and the monarchy together indicate the two poles between which the Dutch state—and probably any state[1]—oscillates. On the one hand, the state in both its legislative and executive organs should reflect the will of the people and, on the other, it should guarantee the continuity of legitimate authority. The first, the "democratic" principle, finds expression in the system of free elections for the national parliament, provincial assemblies, and municipal councils. The second, the "authoritarian" principle, is realized in a triad of offices parallel to the three elected bodies: the monarch, the provincial governor (the "Queen's Commissary"), and the municipal mayor or burgomaster. Both the provincial governor and the burgomaster are appointed by the central government for a six-year term that is normally renewed. Both offices are therefore invested with a built-in stability; in addition, they constitute important links connecting the central government with the provinces and the municipalities.

The continuously expanding administrative apparatus of government in all its ramifications constitutes another element propitious to maintaining a stable authority, the more so since all civil servants hold permanent positions. Ultimately every branch of government is under the supervision of a minister who is responsible to parliament; but the complexity of bureaucracy often reduces the efficacy of parliamentary control.

In the past hundred years, the government apparatus has expanded at an ever faster rate. The number of public employees has grown from 20,000 in 1850 to 400,000 in 1955, or from 1.6 per cent to 9.5 per cent of the total labor force. Concurrently, the percentage of national income devoted to government expenditures rose from 5 per cent in 1850 to 10 per cent in 1900, to 15 per cent in 1930, and to 25 per cent in 1960. These figures clearly mark the increasing amount of state intervention in society. Established departments have expanded, and new ones have been added.[2]

In the days of the Dutch Republic, the central government was expected to deal primarily with international diplomacy and defense; domestic matters were left largely to the provinces and towns. The scope of the central government has widened considerably since, but foreign relations and military defense continue to loom large among its activities; together they still account for one-fifth of the total budget. It is no accident that the term "The Netherlands" may denote the society at large or merely the state or, even more narrowly, the government. In its diplomatic and military functions, the state is the most obvious exponent of the Dutch nation: It guards the frontiers, it issues national passports, it commits the entire people to binding treaties, and leads them into peace or war. The military forces may not be as popular and as conspicuously present as in some other countries; still, they put the very noticeable claim of one and a half year's service upon every male citizen. The general effects of conscription have not yet been studied, but surely the mustering of young men from every social background can hardly fail to have some conforming impact.[3]

Of the two functions, defense and diplomacy, the latter appears to be the most specifically important for Dutch society. The Netherlands has always been a small state, representing but a small territory and a small people. For a while in the seventeenth century the Dutch Republic, led by the province of Holland, rose to great maritime power. In the long run, however, national resources proved too limited for the Netherlands to play a prominent role on the international scene. Ever since the eighteenth century the principal aim of Dutch foreign policy has been to maintain independence and to protect overseas trade and settlements. The means chosen to achieve this aim was the pursuit of neutrality through a reliance upon the balance of power among the larger states of Western Europe.[4] For more than two centuries successive Dutch governments have cultivated a peaceable role in foreign relations. As a result, a mediatory tradition has developed, which has been carried over into domestic politics and into public life in general. Even in cases of profound controversy, the contending parties usually manage to reach some sort of workable compromise; and once an issue has been settled in this way, people tend to abide by the decision. Violence in public life occurs very rarely—the last political murder in national history was committed in 1672.

The maintenance of law and order and the settlement of legal disputes used to be mainly a matter for provincial and town authorities in the old Dutch Republic; only after the foundation of the unitary state did it become of direct concern to the central government. There is now virtually one body of law for the whole country, and equal administration of justice everywhere. In every town the police force is responsible (either directly or indirectly, through the local burgomaster) to the Minister of Domestic Affairs in The Hague; the municipal councils have no say in police matters. On the whole, in keeping law and order, the state leans toward the principle of "authority" rather than "democracy." There is no trial by jury; verdicts in court are given by judges who have been appointed for life by the central government. These arrangements leave little or no scope for direct popular influence either on the way the courts are composed or on their procedures.

There are, however, some counterbalances. The judiciary is always bound by the law as accepted by parliament; it cannot, as in the United States, declare a law unconstitutional and thus supersede parliament. The law as such guarantees a number of civil rights, such as freedom of opinion and speech, freedom of the press, freedom of religion, the free choice of schools, and the right of free association. Also, in accordance with these rights, the police may not make unwarranted arrests or searches. All civil rights are shared equally by all citizens; the judiciary may not discriminate on the grounds of race, creed, or wealth. It is entitled to interfere only when it considers that abuse of civil rights has led to violation of the law, as in libel. As a final check on the administration of justice, court sessions are open to the public and the press.

In the twentieth century the range of formal rights and duties in the relationship between state and individual has widened greatly. In addition to the already established *civil* rights, *political* rights were gradually extended to the whole population; since 1919, when female suffrage was granted, all Dutchmen who have come of age have the right to vote and to run for public office. As a further step toward democratization, the state became charged with the

provision of *social* rights.[5] Today it guarantees a minimum
income to every citizen by supplying old age pensions,
widow's and orphan's pensions, family allowances, and insurance benefits in case of sickness, disability, or unemployment. It sets minimum standards of housing and food
and sees to it that these standards are met. By inspection it
ensures that conditions of work fulfill basic requirements
of safety and hygiene. It sponsors a system of medical care
covering health insurance for all wage earners below a certain income level—this scheme includes about three-
fourths of the population. The state further provides
school education at minimal costs, and it grants scholar-
ships if necessary. All these arrangements are not regarded
as acts of charity that might be revoked at will, but as in-
alienable attributes of social justice.

The introduction of social rights has necessarily cur-
tailed many former liberties. Most notably, the free market economy and the contractual system have been en-
croached upon by a host of legal and administrative
restrictions. The examples by which the Swedish econo-
mist Gunnar Myrdal has indicated the regulatory force of
the state in modern Western society fit the Dutch case
very well.

*The sanctity of private property rights to do what one
pleases with a piece of land; or the right to keep all, except a nominal tax charge, of one's income and wealth
for private consumption or investment; the freedom to
enter upon any profession one wants at one's own risk;
the right of the employer to negotiate individually with
his workers, to pay the smallest salary he can for the
job, and to hire and fire whom he wants, when he
wants; the right of the worker to leave the shop, as and
when he desires; indeed, the free choice to own, acquire
and dispose, to work or to rest, to invest, to trade, to*

*move—all these time-honored individual liberties are
gradually eaten away by the controls of organized society.*[6]

Closely linked with social legislation is the rapidly expanding field of economic legislation. In the Netherlands,
as elsewhere, the disruptions of the two World Wars and
the Great Depression have given rise to protective and coordinating measures aimed at reinforcing the national
economy. Especially after 1945, the government has as-
sumed an active role. Of old the Dutch economy had re-
lied largely on exports, but the damages sustained because
of the German occupation and the loss of the colonial empire in Indonesia were felt to have weakened the export
capacity to such an extent that only a concerted and
guided effort of the whole nation could bring relief. The
response was a deliberate governmental policy attempting
at the same time to keep costs and prices at a low, compet-
itive level and to stimulate continuous investment for industrial expansion. Only in this way, it was felt, could full
employment and prosperity be attained.[7]

The result, as in most Western societies today, is a form
of mitigated free enterprise. The state operates the main
public utility services such as the water, gas, and electricity works, the combined post, telegraph, and telephone
union, and most local transport systems; it owns the quasi-
independent railroad and several coal-mining companies;
and it participates in a few other big companies whose
activities are considered to be of national interest. Otherwise the economy is "free," in the sense that it is run by
private individuals and corporations. The government,
however, possesses many means to influence the entire
economic situation decisively: it can employ direct financial measures in the form of taxes and bonuses; it can
bring about fluctuations in the rate of interest on capital;

it can (though imperfectly) regulate the level of wages, prices, and rents; it can supply or withhold essential permits and facilities; and it can manipulate its own huge expenditures in order to enlarge employment or to check inflationary tendencies. Within the total design of growth for the national economy, the government has promoted schemes of regional development intended to spread industry and commerce more evenly over the whole country and to stimulate new economic developments in specially designated "problem areas." Furthermore, it has protected some of the most vulnerable sectors of the economy, notably agriculture, but also fishing and some languishing manufacturing industries. The forces of the free market have often proved very resilient to attempts at state interference. This has become particularly manifest in the area of housing and real estate, where a twenty-year sequence of government measures like rent restriction and rationed allocation of building permits has not resulted in sufficient relief of a housing shortage that is generally felt to be a pressing national problem.

By contrast, the economic policy of postwar Dutch governments has yielded remarkable results in the field of labor relations and wage control. Since 1945, the guiding principle was to attain close cooperation between the government and organized labor and organized management. An elaborate machinery of joint consultation and control was established, including such organs as the Foundation of Labor, the Board of Government Mediators, and the Social Economic Council.[8] In the immediate post-war era the government, after consulting with the trade unions and the employers' associations, would lay down uniform wage rates for all industries. After 1954, the binding character of national wage policy was gradually relaxed. But while the government has reduced its role as a bargaining partner in negotiations, it still retains the power to overrule any wage proposal deemed undesirable for the national interest. Although in its actual operations the system of joint consultation has changed considerably under successive governments, the underlying principle of seeking voluntary cooperation from management and labor has remained unaltered. For many years the system contributed to keeping wages and prices in the Netherlands at a comparatively low level, and it continues to be successful in maintaining a rather peaceful industrial climate.

Not only do organized labor and management take part in designing social and economic policy, the implementation of that policy is also partly delegated to them. Thus, the administration of social insurance of workers is in the hands of a semi-public body which is neither a "state" nor a "private" organization. In almost every area of social life, such intermediary organizations are proliferating, in the form both of advisory bodies trying to influence the government and of policy-making organs that derive authority from their official state-sponsored character. The symbiotic relationship of free associations, interest groups, and quasi-public corporations *with* the state increasingly binds many segments of society into one close-knit national framework.[9]

Political Parties[10]

So far the state has appeared as a more or less autonomous organization, harmoniously fitting into Dutch society. In a way this is a valid picture: The ubiquitous impact of the state is accepted at least to the extent that revolutions or secessions are never attempted. Underlying this ultimate consensus, however, is a wide array of diverging views as to what the state really should and should not do; the expression of these views may range from articulate opposition to vague discontent. The state is, and always has been, the object of controversy and strain. In the orderly setting of Dutch society, the conflicting views about its functions and authority are represented by established political organizations: by parties primarily and also by pressure groups. These organizations shape the dispersed opinions and demands held by various sectors of the population and carry them onto the national stage.

The legitimate public meeting-ground for political contests is the parliament, especially its most important house, the Second Chamber. This Chamber consists of 150 members, chosen by the people and representing different parties. Elections for the Chamber are national: Each party receives a number of seats proportional to the total number of votes it has collected throughout the country. This system of proportional representation virtually converts the whole nation into one constituency, and thus weakens the basis for regional identification in national politics. Since it also encumbers the growth of strong personal links between a deputy and his constituents, the system reinforces the power of the central party bureau which draws up the lists of candidates. All parties therefore operate on a wide national basis, even if they have particular regional strongholds in their following. The same holds true for the various pressure groups representing the interests of farming, industry, and trade: They also concentrate their activities upon the center of national politics in The Hague.

The era between 1870 and 1920 was the formative period of modern Dutch politics. Within that half century, as the state made ever deeper inroads into society, the gradually enfranchised masses were rallied into political movements aiming to check and to direct the state's expanding powers. Three issues dominated this crucial epoch: the extension of suffrage, the so-called schools issue, and the "social problem." The extension of the suffrage proceeded rapidly—from 11.3 per cent of all adult men in 1870, to 12.3 per cent in 1880, 26.8 per cent in 1890, 49.0 per cent in 1900, and 63.2 per cent in 1910; finally, in 1917 the franchise was extended to all men above twenty-five, and two years later to women as well.[11] This momentous development gradually changed the power structure in parliament and destroyed the undisputed leadership of the liberal burgher elite. New interests calling attention to the schools issue and the social problem made themselves heard. The alignments evolving around these questions have determined the fourfold division of parties that has dominated Dutch politics until today. The schools issue became acute with the extension of public education to the masses; it centered around the demand made by the Roman Catholics and the Orthodox Protestants that the state should support schools of specific religious denominations on an equal basis with the non-denominational schools, a demand which put them in opposition to the more secular-minded Protestant Liberals. The second dominating issue concerned the question of whether the state should initiate social legislation to protect the workers in the rapidly spreading industrial system. The debate on this issue has produced considerable tension within the confessional parties and has given rise to a large Socialist party confronting the Liberals in the nonconfessional quarter. Today's party structure still evolves around the same two axes: confessional versus nonconfessional on the one hand, and liberal versus socialist on the other. Since both axes constitute varieties of the right-left dimension, the actual distinction between right and left may vary depending upon the issue at stake.

Table 5 indicates the division of seats in the Second Chamber of parliament since 1888. It lists no less than six parties, but even this listing is a simplification. Some of the figures quoted are compounds for two or more separate parties which have been taken together for the sake of convenience; thus the 47 Socialist seats for 1963 are divided into 43 for the Labor party and 4 for the Pacifist Socialists. The parties are grouped under two headings: "Nonconfessional" and "Confessional." The major nonconfessional parties are the economically conservative Liberals (the *Volkspartij voor Vrijheid en Democratie,* or VVD), the Socialists (the *Partij van de Arbeid,* or PvdA), and the Communists (the *Communistische Partij Nederland,* or CPN); the major confessional parties are the Roman Catholics (the *Katholieke Volkspartij,* or KVP) and the two related Protestant parties, the Anti-Revolutionary party (ARP—the name expresses a stand against the secular impact of the French Revolution) and the Christian Historical Union (CHU—a politically rather nondescript group with conservative leanings attached by sentiment to the Dutch Reformed Church). The residual column of "Others" comprises various minor parties, some confessional and some nonconfessional, some right-wing and some left-wing, and most short-lived.[12]

Claiming to embody "the thinking part of the nation," the Liberals dominated Dutch politics until the turn of the century. With the extension of the franchise they had to yield their majority to the confessional parties, which together have collected more than half of the votes ever since 1901. On the whole, the stability of the Dutch electorate during the past fifty years has been remarkable. Each election has brought some slight shifts, but the reciprocal gains and losses never amounted to more than a few seats. One reason for this stability may be the leveling effects of proportional representation introduced together with universal suffrage in 1917. Another may be that in this same year registration at the polls was made compulsory, a circumstance that may have caused a regular percentage of votes to be cast by people who do not keep

TABLE 5

Division of Seats in the
Second Chamber of Parliament, 1888–1963

Election Year	Party										Total
	Liberals	Social-ists	Commu-nists	Total Non-confes-sional	Roman Cath-olics	ARP	CHU	Total Confes-sional	Others		Total
1888	46	1	—	47	25	27	—	52	1		100
1891	54	—	—	54	25	21	—	46	—		100
1894	60	—	—	60	25	15	—	40	—		100
1897	52	2	—	54	22	17	6	45	1		100
1901	35	6	—	41	25	23	9	57	2		100
1905	45	6	—	51	25	15	8	48	1		100
1909	33	7	—	40	25	25	10	60	—		100
1913	39	15	—	54	25	11	10	46	—		100
1918	20	22	2	46	30	13	7	50	4		100

1922	15	20	2	37	32	16	11	59	4	100
1925	16	24	1	41	30	13	11	54	5	100
1929	15	24	2	41	30	12	11	53	6	100
1933	13	22	4	39	28	14	10	52	9	100
1937	10	23	3	36	31	17	8	56	8	100
1946	6	29	10	45	32	13	8	53	2	100
1948	8	27	8	43	32	13	9	54	3	100
1952	9	30	6	45	30	12	9	51	4	100
1956	9	34	4	47	33	10	8	51	2	100
1956*	13	50	7	70	49	15	13	77	3	150
1959	19	50	3	72	49	14	12	75	3	150
1963	16	47	4	67	50	13	13	76	7	150

* In 1956, the number of seats was increased from 100 to 150.
SOURCE: Netherlands Central Bureau of Statistics, *Election Statistics*.

abreast of political developments. The most important explanation, however, lies no doubt in the very nature of Dutch political parties, which do not appeal merely to the voter's opinion on current political issues but to his basic religious and moral commitments. As the Dutch political scientist Hans Daalder has put it:

> The great debate is that between the religious and the nonreligious parties, the one group denying the other's raison d'être. The Liberals and the Partij van de Arbeid argue that members of different religious communions may perfectly well share the same political opinions, that while an individual's religious and political convictions may be closely related, no such relation is necessary in the nation at large, and that, indeed, a relation between religion and politics at the national level is detrimental to both because it exposes religion to the vagaries of ephemeral political passions while it confuses political issues by introducing irrelevant religious considerations. The religious parties, on the other hand, claim that politics is not something separate and purely temporal but something to be subordinated to eternal values. Religious parties, they claim, are natural and rightful parties, and any political differences there may be should be settled by discussions and compromise within religious positions.[13]

Despite the numerical stability of election results, notable changes have taken place in the working relationships among the parties. There has been a definite rapprochement along both axes of the political system. The three competing emancipationist movements, the Roman Catholics, the Orthodox Protestants, and the Socialists, have each secured an established power position which they safeguard by maintaining the total balance of Dutch politics; on this basis of common interest they cooperate, respecting each other as both rivals and partners. Antagonism between confessional and nonconfessional parties lost its sharpest edges as early as 1916, when the schools issue was settled with full financial state aid to all denominational schools. During the nineteen twenties and thirties the deepest cleavage existed between the Socialists and the other parties. The majority of the Socialists in this period persisted in a radical rejection of capitalist society, including the monarchy and the churches. Only gradually did a more accommodating attitude grow on both sides, and it was not until 1939 that a Socialist joined the cabinet—in this respect the Netherlands lagged far behind all other countries of Western Europe. After the Second World War rapprochement continued more rapidly. It was furthered by the increasing amount of social and economic legislation on which practically all parties found themselves compelled to agree in order not to alienate a substantial number of voters. Party programs on social and economic policy have converged a great deal, although the Liberals and the Socialists especially still quarrel over any issue concerning the distribution of income and wealth. In the debates, the Liberals emphasize individual responsibility, whereas the Socialists stress the need for collective provisions. The confessional parties follow a middle course, trying to keep internal equilibrium by not leaning too far in either direction. Once a bill has been accepted, all parties will tend to subscribe to it, thus confirming J. K. Galbraith's observation that "one of the most surprising features of social welfare legislation is its inability to sustain controversy after it has been passed into law." [14]

Parliamentary life is characterized by a mixture of doctrinal dispute and practical collaboration. Since no single party can attain an absolute majority, every cabinet perforce consists of a coalition in which several parties are represented. Theoretically it is always possible to form a coalition of the confessional parties, but such a coalition would probably be impracticable for lack of internal coherence. Since 1946, therefore, the final outcome has invariably been a cabinet consisting of a Roman Catholic center, usually supplemented by one or both Protestant parties, and completed alternately with Liberals or Socialists.

Because of the frequent two-way traffic between government and opposition, none of the major parties ever assumes the role of either an all-out government or an all-out opposition party. The cabinets on their part tend to take an above-party attitude, as if they were serving the national interest in an objective manner transcending the segmental interests represented by the parties. Obviously this imparts the position of a cabinet minister with role-conflict: loyalty is demanded both by his party and by the coalition. Usually the claims of ministerial responsibility are the stronger and he may then become estranged from his political associates in parliament. It is significant that the Roman Catholics especially have at times kept their most prominent men away from government posts in order to save them for parliamentary leadership considered of greater value to the party.

All these conditions combine to make the formation of a cabinet in most cases a long and arduous process. A new cabinet can make its appearance only after full agreement has been reached by all participants with regard to the program as well as to the personal distribution of offices; this may take several weeks or even months of negotiations. The very delicacy of its formation lends to each cabinet a certain invulnerability: no one is anxious to jeopardize a structure so painstakingly put together. This reinforces the tendency of the cabinet to face parliament as a separate and independent body. It is revealing of the detachment between cabinet and parliament that almost two-thirds of all ministers since 1848 had not been members of parliament before they first acceded to their post: Government and politics are somehow regarded as separate areas. (On a different level, but also significant, is the formal rule of etiquette that requires ministers to be addressed as "Your Excellency," while the members of parliament must settle for a plain "Mister.") Because of the vast complexity of government, the ascendancy of the cabinet over parliament has tended to increase in recent years. Ministerial authority is high; even if a minister happens to be widely regarded as of little personal consequence, his office still carries considerable prestige and power.

The whole process of cabinet formation takes place beyond direct popular control. The people elect only the parliamentary representatives to whom the government to be formed after the election will be responsible. Most of these representatives are not elected as persons but as candidates on a party slate. And since each party will be able to carry out its platform only after many mutual concessions, the voter does not even give his mandate to a clear-cut program of policy; he merely endorses the general principles the party stands for. Thus the rigidity of the political structure is enhanced by the formal arrangements of the electoral system. It would be an interesting experiment to see if a reform in these formal arrangements would disturb the stability of party relationships.

As it is, the polls yield few surprises and, accordingly, rouse little excitement. An electoral survey held during the national election campaigns of 1956 in the municipality of Nieuwer Amstel near Amsterdam brought to light gross indifference and lack of knowledge.[15] Only 5 per cent of the respondents stated that they were very interested in the election, 35 per cent were moderately interested, and 59 per cent were not interested at all. The de-

gree of involvement in the campaigns was generally low.
More than half of the respondents never discussed politics
at home, at work, or with friends. No less than 60 per
cent could not mention any issue on which the different
parties strongly disagreed. Against this background it is
hardly surprising that 85 per cent of the respondents
voted for the same party in 1956 as they had in 1952.
Stability was highest among the Roman Catholics (92
per cent) and the *Gereformeerden* (94 per cent), and lowest among the nonreligious (74 per cent). The Roman
Catholics and the *Gereformeerden* also came nearest to
complete identification with one particular political party,
with 85 per cent of the Roman Catholics voting KVP and
as many *Gereformeerden* voting ARP. The Christian Historical Union appears to recruit most of its voters from
members of the Dutch Reformed Church, but it does not
monopolize them to the same degree: Dutch Reformed
voters are divided about equally over PvdA and CHU,
and to a slightly less extent over VVD. (See Table 6).

As suggested by Table 7, the main parties exhibit on
the whole a great similarity in the economic background

TABLE 6

*Denominational Structure of the Following of the
Main Political Parties, Nieuwer Amstel, 1956*

	Religious Denomination (per cent)						
Party	Roman Catholic	Dutch Reformed	Gerefor- meerd	Others	None	No Reply	Total
KVP	95	1	—	—	1	3	100
PvdA	4	44	2	5	42	3	100
ARP	2	17	74	1	3	3	100
CHU	—	89	1	2	2	6	100
VVD	7	46	2	3	38	4	100

SOURCE: *Kiezer en Verkiezing,* mimeographed report of the Nieuwer Amstel Survey, Institute of Political Science, University of
Amsterdam, 1963, p. 22.

of their adherents.[16] The only exception is the VVD, which has a predominantly wealthier following. Interest-

TABLE 7

Income Structure of the Following of the Main Political Parties, Nieuwer Amstel, 1956

	Income (per cent)				
Party	Less Than Dutch fl. 6,000*	Dutch fl. 6,000– 10,000	More Than Dutch fl. 10,000	No Reply	Total
KVP	66	16	9	9	100
PvdA	67	18	6	9	100
ARP	62	22	7	9	100
CHU	68	15	6	11	100
VVD	29	34	27	10	100

* One Dutch florin (guilder) = 27.6 cents.
SOURCE: *Kiezer en Verkiezing,* mimeographed report of the Nieuwer Amstel Survey, Institute of Political Science, University of Amsterdam, 1963, p. 29.

ingly, the percentage of confessional voters among the religious respondents decreases slightly as one moves up the scale of occupational prestige and income. This finding suggests that the various blocs tend to be more "closed" at the bottom and "open" at the top. It appears to reflect the corporate character of the religious emancipation movements: In politics, the Roman Catholics and the *Gereformeerden* have achieved national integration through collective effort, and it is only through their own collectivity that the majority of believers feel connected with the larger political community. Among those, however, who by virtue of a higher socioeconomic position have a wider choice of social and cultural opportunities, the range of political options tends to increase as well.

All major political organizations can count on a solid mass of followers. They all operate on a national scale, and they are all well engrained in the existing national order. At the extremes of the political spectrum there are a number of small radical parties which display greater militancy; altogether they have seldom obtained more than 10 per cent of the votes. In the spring 1966 elections for the provincial assemblies this rule was broken, as considerable gains went to two "outsiders," the Pacifist Socialists and the populist Farmers Party. Although this was widely regarded as a most disturbing result, it still left more than 80 per cent of the votes to the five center parties. The various pressure groups promoting or defending particular interests also tend to respect and stabilize the established political relationships—far from upsetting the prevailing structure they take care to plant their representatives into each major party. Thus the most striking feature of the Dutch political scene remains its tranquillity. For the time being, the majority of the Dutch electorate and its leaders appear to have settled firmly in the fourfold division dictated by the principles of *verzuiling*.

The Educational System

Schools dominate the lives of more than a quarter of the Dutch population—all children between the ages of six and fourteen, a great many adolescents and young adults up to the age of twenty-five or even thirty, and the teachers, who make up about 2 per cent of the Dutch labor force. Economically, formal education is a gigantic concern. In the national state budget it ranks first, with almost a quarter of the government expenditures; and to this might be added all the contingent costs paid by parents for their school-going children, plus the potential earnings foregone for the sake of studying.

The great social importance of schools is a rather recent phenomenon. Traditionally the foremost social function of education has been to transmit the culture of a society to the younger generation in such a way that its members are prepared in time to take their appropriate places in the social structure. This mainly conservative function once required but limited formal instruction; only a hundred years ago about 25 per cent of Dutch children did not go to school at all—home and the local community provided all the education thought necessary for them to reach their designated social station. Modernization has thoroughly changed these conditions. No longer does education culminate in handing down the wisdom of the past to those considered fit to inherit it; increasingly the schools are used to raise the general level of culture from one generation to another by imparting newly acquired knowledge and skills, by opening up new channels of recruitment, and by prolonging the over-all learning period. Along with this changing cultural function, formal education has also taken on a new structural function: It is becoming the principal means for the allocation of personnel in the occupational world, thus promoting, from a societal point of view, the mobilization of talent, and, from the individual point of view, social mobility.

In its present shape the Dutch educational system may be regarded as an exemplary manifestation of both national unity and uniqueness. It is a unity because in all its ramifications it is subsidized by the national government and, consequently, subject to uniform standards and arrangements enforced by the Ministry of Education. At the same time, in spite of extensive borrowings from foreign models, it is unique in its organizational structure, didactic methods, and contents of curriculum. Unity is greatest at the level of the elementary school, which therefore functions as a most important agency for the transmission of national culture. Here all children from six to twelve learn to read and write the Dutch language—a basic prerequisite for participating in the national community. They also learn arithmetic, a less nation-bound subject, but no less indispensable in modern society. History and geography are taught again from a pronouncedly national viewpoint, with particular reference to the Dutch scene. Then there are standard songs, stories, and rules of behavior which also contribute to the national homogeneity of all Dutch children. The elementary school reaches into every social milieu; for many pupils in rural areas or working class neighborhoods it establishes the first personal encounter with urban middle-class culture. For some, this encounter may eventually lead to social mobility and cultural assimilation, while the majority will at least be influenced toward greater cultural uniformity. The total impact of the elementary school is hard to measure, but it is undoubtedly great. For at least six years all children are exposed to the same curriculum and the same discipline. During this period a standard minimum of common culture is inculcated in them, in the form of knowledge as well as manners and morals.

The elementary school is followed by a wide array of secondary schools. Unlike the single comprehensive high school in the United States, there are many different types of schools which may be classified into a few general levels, more or less unequivocally graded by intellectual rigor and social prestige. Thus, in the 1960 census the Dutch adult working population was found to be composed as follows (it should be noted that the percentages refer to the active breadwinners, most of whom are men; the educational level of the adult population as a whole is lower):

51.6 per cent have only attained the elementary level of primary school, either with or without one or two years of unfinished further training (this includes also ap-

proximately 10 *per cent who have not been able to complete primary school.*)

33.5 *per cent have received a full technical or clerical education at the* lower secondary level, *usually extending three or four years beyond the sixth form of elementary school.*

7.1 *per cent have finished an education at the* higher secondary level, *equivalent to at least five or six years beyond the sixth form; from this level one may go on to either of the two following.*

1.9 *per cent have proceeded beyond the higher secondary level to the* higher vocational level, *generally requiring another three or four years and roughly equivalent to the completion of an American college training.*

1.4 *per cent have continued their studies beyond the higher secondary level at an institute of higher learning and have after a period of from five to ten years obtained a degree at the* academic or university level.[17]

The different types of schools are agencies both of selection and of differentiation. Each school attracts a fairly homogeneous population of students already sharing similar capacities and interests. The process of selection does not stop at first admittance but goes on from day to day; those who do not live up to the school's standards will fail and will eventually drop out. At the same time the school continues to cultivate the very same qualities that guide the selection process, such as technical competence in the trade schools and linguistic ability in the classically oriented *gymnasiums;* progress is regularly examined and rated in report cards. Moreover, apart from the formally prescribed knowledge and skills, each school tends to pass on to its students a set of congruous cultural values and social manners. Formally these two functions of purely "technical" and wider "social" teaching may be separated, but in reality they are heavily contingent. Thus, the better command of language attained through study at the higher secondary level of a *gymnasium* is not merely a scholastic accomplishment but an invaluable social asset as well, marking a person as being "educated" and thus raising his social credit.

It is no wonder, then, that the stratification of schools into different levels runs closely parallel to the stratification of occupations on the basis of social prestige as described on page 67. Holders of a university degree belong almost without exception to the highest prestige stratum; their rank is accentuated by the widespread custom of using academic titles ostentatiously. A few of those who have finished a higher secondary or vocational education may also reach stratum I, but the majority will find an occupation ranked in stratum II. The lower secondary level will lead in most cases to either stratum III or IV, while those who have not gone beyond the elementary level will be confined to strata IV, V, and VI.[18]

Since 1901, when elementary education was made compulsory for all children between six and twelve, school attendance has become virtually universal. There are no problems of widespread truancy; most parents accept their legal obligation as a social necessity. Successive revisions of the law have raised the minimum school-leaving age to fifteen, while at the same time voluntary enrollment in secondary schools has greatly increased. In 1850, it has been estimated, only 95 out of every 1,000 boys in the age category of twelve to seventeen attended a secondary school; in 1930 this number had risen to 196; in 1947, to 394; and in 1961, to 635. A continuous upgrading of the educational level is going on; each new age cohort enters the labor force with better educational equipment than its predecessor. Between 1930 and 1960 the number of uni-

versity graduates has tripled; taking the general population growth into account, this still means a proportional
increase of almost 100 per cent from one generation to the
next.[19]

With the expansion of secondary and higher education,
the scope of recruitment has widened. A university training is no longer the exclusive privilege of the sons of the
well-to-do elite. But neither has it yet become an inaliena-
ble right enjoyed as a matter of course by all who wish
and warrant it because of their innate capacities. Formally
the educational system offers equal opportunities to everyone; but some inveterate social and cultural obstacles
block the realization of this democratic tenet. One of these
obstacles used to be religion; and although they are rapidly catching up, the Roman Catholics are still underrepresented at the universities, in contrast to the unchurchly
and the members of the "other" denominations, who contribute more than their relative share to the student population. Likewise the western provinces and the cities are
still ahead of the rest of the country; but these differences,
too, grow smaller each year. Also liable to decrease but
still very large at present is the inequality in educational
enrollment of boys and girls. This inequality runs through
all sections of the population, and manifests itself in every
type of school. At the universities, where the differences
stand out most clearly, the ratio of male versus female students is still about 5 to 1.[20]

Most noticeable are the disparities between the socioeconomic strata. In the academic year 1945–1955, university
enrollment in the age bracket from eighteen to twenty-
nine was 1.4 per cent for the whole population; broken
down according to the occupational strata of the parents,
the percentages were 8.9 for strata I and II, 1.5 for strata
III and IV, and 0.2 for strata V and VI. These figures
have not altered significantly; today the two lowest strata,

comprising about two-fifths of the Dutch population, still contribute less than 10 per cent to the total number of university students.[21] Exact comparative data are hard to give, but it seems that the lower strata in the Netherlands avail themselves of educational opportunities to a lesser degree than in most other Western European countries. There can be no doubt that in this respect the Netherlands is far behind the United States.[22]

The inequalities manifested at the university level are reflected throughout the educational system. Even in the first form of elementary school, children from different socioeconomic backgrounds begin to diverge in scholastic achievements. Obviously, at this level financial difficulties cannot play much part; the causes are much more likely to be found in a social and cultural cleavage between the school and the home and neighborhood of the children from the lower strata. There is increasing evidence that the dissociation between these two environments lies at the root of many scholastic failures. Probably in the Netherlands, as well as in Great Britain, working-class children are handicapped because they have not learned to master a "formal" language before they enter school;[23] lacking this, they have trouble understanding the lessons and fulfilling the required tasks. To this linguistic barrier may be added other adverse influences springing from the home environment in the way of indifferent or even inimical attitudes toward the school and the learning and respectability it represents.[24]

While socioeconomic class differences continue to impinge upon education, inversely, education is becoming an increasingly important determinant of socioeconomic class position. The complex modern industrial organizations and the rapidly growing tertiary sector of the economy demand qualified personnel, especially in executive positions. For the higher-salaried and prestige-carrying technical, managerial, and professional occupations, an education at a medium secondary level at the very least is required, and a university degree is becoming increasingly advisable. Schools, therefore, have gained greatly in importance as sorting agencies in the allocation of socioeconomic status. The national system of government-certified diplomas reinforces this sorting function. It articulates a hierarchy of "lower, middle, and higher" learning, with minute subdivisions. The position one has reached upon this scale bears heavily upon one's occupational opportunities. In industry, and even more in the civil service, careers move to a large extent between limits set by the educational certificates. Advertisements offering vacancies usually specify precisely the required level of education; anyone below this level need not apply. The very ambitious who lack the proper school training have only one way left: to improve their educational status through self-study or extension courses. Thus a similar situation obtains in the Netherlands that has been described by the British sociologist T. H. Marshall:

> Great and increasing respect is paid to certificates, matriculation, degrees and diplomas as qualifications for employment, and their freshness does not fade with the passage of the years. A man of forty may be judged by his performance in an examination taken at the age of fifteen. The ticket obtained on leaving school or college is for a life journey.[25]

At the same time that diplomas become more indispensable they are also losing their relative value. Not only does the modern economy require specially trained technical and social skills; it also seeks diplomas, because they offer ready standard information about a man's abilities regardless of his personal background, and they thus facilitate the speed and the desired neutrality of the selection process. Thus the demand for diplomas has risen for several reasons. In response, the schools have produced more graduates, but this greater supply has inevitably made for a general devaluation of diplomas.[26] Competition is continuously pushed up to higher levels of qualification; there appears to be a self-propelling force in the pressure toward more education somewhat reminiscent of Parkinson's law of bureaucratic growth.

The graded school system, by setting uniform and generally accepted educational standards, promotes the national unity of Dutch society. At the same time, by applying these standards, it effectively differentiates the population into various distinct educational levels. A similarly double effect of integration and differentiation is produced by the tripartition of the Dutch school system along the lines of religious confession.

At each level, from the nursery school to the university, parents may choose among three sorts of schools: the neutral public school, the confessional Protestant school, and the confessional Roman Catholic school. Since 1920 all of these schools have received full financial support from the state. The public schools are administered by the municipal town boards, the confessional schools by private boards. As the supplier of the material means, the state imposes binding conditions upon all schools regarding such matters as admittance, curriculum, degrees, number of teachers, qualifications of teachers, and so forth. Owing to the general arrangements incorporating all schools into one system, the Ministry of Education can guarantee that the various institutions at each level meet equivalent standards of scholastic performance.

Apart from the officially prescribed standards, however, the confessional and the public schools diverge in several ways. As is to be expected, the differences occur primarily in the religious teaching—biblical knowledge and articles of faith—but the dissimilarities extend into other subjects as well. In history, for example, the view presented in Roman Catholic schools of the Dutch revolt against Spain and the concurrent Protestantization of society deviates on critical points from the "public" or Protestant version. There are even some striking cases of typically Roman Catholic idiom in the Dutch language, due to the wording of the catechism taught in Roman Catholic classes. Yet more important than the varied cultural content of the teaching is the social isolation caused by segmental education. Every child spends a large part of the day in an insular environment where contacts are virtually restricted to members of the same confessional or nonconfessional bloc.[27]

The introduction of financial parity in 1920 has greatly benefited the confessional schools. In 1900, 69 per cent of all children in elementary schools went to a public school and only 31 per cent to another type of school; in 1920 this ratio had become 55 to 45; in 1930, 38 to 62; in 1950, 27 to 73; and in 1962, 26 to 74. Of the latter 74 per cent, about 2 per cent went to nondenominational neutral private schools, and the remaining 72 per cent to confessional Roman Catholic and Protestant schools. This figure gives a slightly exaggerated indication of the degree of "confessionalization" among the adult population, inasmuch as it leaves out the number of children per family, which is comparatively high among the Roman Catholics and the *Gereformeerden*. Taking family size into account, the Dutch sociologist J. P. Kruijt has calculated that in 1957, 35 per cent of all parents sent their children to a Roman Catholic elementary school, 28 per cent to a Protestant one, and 37 per cent to a neutral one. This would mean that approximately 90 per cent of the Roman Catholic and *Gereformeerde* parents, 50 per cent of the Dutch Reformed and "others," and 10 per cent of the nonchurchly chose a confessional elementary school for their children.[28] Thus the schools, while embracing the entire Dutch youth within one national system, also serve to perpetuate the distinctions connected with *verzuiling* as well as with socioeconomic status.

Finally, it is worth noting that the percentage of Roman Catholic and Protestant students attending confessional schools decreases steadily as one moves up to higher levels of the educational system. This can be partly explained on the grounds of exigency, for in many areas the total number of students does not warrant a tripartition of advanced schools, so that one simply has no choice. But in addition, the same principle appears to be at work that has been brought to light in electoral surveys; namely, that the confessional blocs tend to be more "closed" at the bottom and "open" at the top. Members of the higher occupational strata and students at the higher educational institutions apparently enjoy a greater leeway in moving outside their denominational bloc.

Socioeconomic Organizations

The economy is a most important factor in the national integration of Dutch society. There are no longer self-sufficient local or family units; every household depends upon a vast network of exchange and is tied to the larger economy by the "cash nexus." Monetarily and fiscally, the Netherlands is a clearly defined whole with one currency and one uniform tax system. Modern industry has increasingly transformed the entire country into one market for its mass products; shops in every region carry the same basic assortment of brands, and the same advertisements present a common frame of reference to all Dutch consumers. Intense competition on a national scale regularly leads to mergers, the result being that increasingly large firms have an ever-larger share of the total market. In addition, all sorts of groups with distinct economic interests, such as workers and employers or producers and consumers, have established central organizations promoting their collective causes on the widest possible national basis. These organizations find themselves sometimes opposed to and sometimes cooperating with the state, which, as pointed out above, is steadily extending its role of coordinating the national economy.

Traditionally, the Dutch economy has always had a strong international orientation; modernization has accentuated this tendency even further. The thriving city of Rotterdam exemplifies the importance of foreign trade; thanks to its huge transit traffic, it is the second largest port in the world. Compared with other European countries, the Netherlands has the highest rate of import and export in relation to national income; in 1963 these rates were 41.4 per cent and 34.4 per cent, respectively.[29] Because of this heavy reliance upon foreign trade, the Dutch economy is particularly sensitive to international trends. Thus the Netherlands shared in the Great Depression of the nineteen thirties, suffered severely from the devastations of World War II, recovered rapidly with the aid of the Marshall Plan between 1945 and 1950, and rose to unprecedented prosperity thereafter. Its intensive involvement in international developments has greatly stimulated the tendency toward increasing national association and control. In addition, this involvement has encouraged a sense of national solidarity and joint responsibility, especially on the part of the labor unions, thus contributing to the relatively quiet industrial relations of the postwar years.

The labor movement had a rather late and timid start in the Netherlands. The first local unions of skilled craftsmen appeared in the eighteen sixties, and only toward the end of the nineteenth century did the movement begin to gain massive support. Almost from the beginning, organized labor was split into different segments according to the familiar Dutch pattern of *verzuiling;* thus, "general," socialist, Protestant, and Roman Catholic unions were founded. The "general" union, guided by close patronage of the employers, proved unviable; the other three variants have continued to exist side by side up to the present day. In the early years conflict between the socialist and the confessional unions often ran high, the socialists favoring radical demands and aggressive tactics and the confessionals taking a far more subdued and generally conservative stand. As in politics, the differences have grown smaller in time, so that today the three movements agree and collaborate on most practical issues. Thus in 1964, the three national federations published a joint scheme for allotting the workers a financial share in the profits of industry.

On the whole the history of the Dutch trade unions is marked by increasing integration into the larger society. In the last decades of the nineteenth century a huge gap loomed between the respectable, well-educated, well-fed and well-dressed bourgeoisie and the poor and often illiterate workers, who possessed neither the political right of suffrage nor any formal social rights. In these conditions the emerging Socialist labor unions strongly opposed the employers and, concomitantly, the entire societal status quo. The fight they put up was often vehement but limited in scope and ephemeral: a strike would break out and perhaps spread to some nearby plants; there might be riots and armed clashes with strikebreakers and policemen. But after some turbulent days or, at most, weeks, the struggle would end in either victory or defeat. The stakes were high; defeat usually implied exclusion and unemployment. In the twentieth century labor conflicts have gradually lost this spontaneous and violent character; the battle scene has shifted from the local to the national front, while direct action has been superseded by collective bargaining. Thus developments in the Netherlands fit well into the general trend toward what the German sociologist Theodor Geiger has called "the institutionalization of class antagonism": The conflicts between labor and management have not disappeared, but both parties have conceded in the acceptance of a set of rules providing for settlement by orderly means.[30] In the Netherlands this development has gone further than in most countries.

A signal event was the passing of the Industrial Disputes Act in 1923, which established a national institution for settling labor conflicts by referring them to a tripartite board of mediators representing the government, the workers, and the employers. Under these arrangements the three largest trade union movements, Socialist, Protestant, and Roman Catholic, were officially recognized as the representatives of labor. Especially since 1945, the central federations of the "recognized" unions, as they are now generally known, have held a very strong negotiating position at the national level. They are the sole representatives of the workers in the Foundation of Labor and the Socioeconomic Council, the two most important advisory bodies on social and economic government policy (see p. 81). In return for this exclusive recognition, they are expected to act "constructively" and "responsibly." Accordingly they have tended to pursue long-range rather than short-range ends, putting matters of national interest such as full employment above incidental advantages for particular groups of workers. In the immediate postwar period of recovery they have helped to maintain a low wage level so as to further industrial investment and to facilitate Dutch competition in the international market. In the years of prosperity following economic recovery they have

perpetuated the same policy of loyalty and restraint, pre-
ferring negotiation to strikes and keeping to the collective
agreements made with government and management.

Their monopoly in the national boards of negotiation
has given the recognized unions a strong voice in the determination of labor conditions in every branch of industry throughout the country. However, bargaining at the
national level with government and management has also
tended to alienate their leaders from the rank-and-file
workers. The individual worker may feel no particular
urge to join a union since his interests are represented
anyway—any improvement secured by the union will au-
tomatically accrue to members and nonmembers alike.
Moreover, in some prosperous industries hard-pressed by a
labor shortage, wage raises that seem easily attainable are
not materializing because the unions reject them as in-
compatible with the public interest. In order to overcome
this latter source of embarrassment, the trade unions and
the organizations of employers have been trying for some
time to shun their third partner, government. As a result,
a less restricted wage system that leaves more scope for
special arrangements in each industry was gradually put
into effect in recent years. Yet the government still re-
serves the authority to overrule any agreement considered
harmful to the economy at large.

The functions of the trade unions are not confined to
bargaining over work conditions; their historical significance is much wider. Along with their struggle on the
economic front, they have greatly contributed to the social
and cultural integration of workers by encouraging self-
confidence and self-discipline, by offering recreational facilities, by pointing the way to educational improvement,
and by providing incentives toward the social advancement of working-class children.[31] Because today the gap
between the middle class and the working class is not as

glaring as it used to be, the integrative functions of the unions have become less spectacular. Yet they still continue—in a wide variety of fields, including leisure, education, social work, public health, and housing.

In some ways the very success of the union movement seems to hamper its further development. For example, the general provision of unemployment benefits by the state has deprived the unions of their insurance function, thus taking away a vital motive for membership. Another problem the unions are facing today is how to attract the steadily growing sector of white collar workers who show, on the whole, little inclination to join one of the established organizations. Altogether the strong position of union leadership in the national advisory and policy-making organs is matched by the incessant problem of gaining sufficient worker support, of overcoming the radical tendencies of some and the indifference of many. Today about one third of all employed workers belong to the recognized unions; another 8 per cent are associated with other unions, and the remainder are not organized at all. Membership turnover tends to be high, and active participation is generally low.[32]

Still, the three recognized federations of trade unions together comprise well over a million members, which makes them by far the largest socioeconomic associations in Dutch society. The employers' organizations, founded in order to present a national counterpart to the government and the trade unions, have a much smaller membership, and so do the organizations of independent retailers and tradesmen and of farmers. But all of these organizations represent smaller social categories than the employed workers; and, although their absolute membership is lower, they rank higher in relative enrollment of potential members. Thus while in 1962 a total of 40 per cent of all employed workers were organized in a union, the ratios for the independent middle class and the farmers were 45 per cent and 75 per cent, respectively.[33]

The highest percentage of membership has been attained by the farmers' unions. As in all Western industrial societies, agriculture in the Netherlands has been facing grave difficulties due to a steadily mounting supply and an inelastic demand for agricultural products. One and the same quandary confronts all farmers; it is no wonder they have united into a vigorous "green front," the most active of all Dutch socioeconomic pressure groups. Although at the moment representing less than 10 per cent of the working population, the farmers' organizations exert great influence within the major political parties as well as in the main advisory bodies concerned with socioeconomic government policy. Their efforts have not relieved Dutch agriculture from its structural problems, but they have succeeded in wresting many compensatory measures. Consequently, the central government now allots more than 500 million guilders ($135 million) per annum in direct support to farming, while consumers contribute a great sum in the form of protected prices that are often considerably above the prices in the world market.[34]

The unions of workers, employers, farmers, and so forth are all voluntary associations; neither in industry nor in agriculture is there anything resembling a "closed shop" system. Since 1938, however, Dutch law provides for the establishment of statutory corporations, membership in which can be made compulsory for everyone engaged in a particular branch of economic activity. Such corporations (*publiekrechtelijke bedrijfsorganen*) have been established especially in those branches where small private enterprise still predominates, such as farming, fishing, and retailing. The corporations, founded either at the request of representatives from the branch concerned or, in a few cases, at the instigation of the national government, are vested with the authority to levy taxes and to issue regulations; both the dues and the rules are compulsory for the whole sector. The actual regulations vary from one corporation to another; usually they relate to such matters as licensing requirements, minimum prices, training and qualifications, wages and other labor conditions, quality of products, normalization of goods and packaging, competition, and discounts. In addition, the corporation renders various services such as carrying out research and disseminating information. The individual entrepreneur has to yield some of his personal freedom in return for the anticipated benefits to be gained when the entire branch is fortified through coordination. Inevitably, these arrangements further the trend toward standardization and greater national uniformity.

Almost all socioeconomic organizations, voluntary as well as statutory, represent the interests of "producers," that is, of people acting in their capacity as earners of an income through either wages or profits. Sometimes these interests are clearly opposed to the interests shared by all members of Dutch society in their economic role of consumers. The situation is very complex: To a certain extent the respective interests run parallel, but there are points where they obviously diverge—for example, when manufacturers enter into a cartel agreement not to sell below a certain price or when resale margins are fixed by "vertical" contracts between producers and retailers. In such cases the Ministry of Economic Affairs may interfere on behalf of the consumer, as it often does, with varying success. However, the government is not the trustee and protector of consumers' interests only; it is also supposed to further the producers' interests, and the various producers' organizations are not lax in stressing this function. In size and efficiency they far outstrip the national consumers' union, which in 1965 had less than 200,000 members. The cause of this disparity, as Gunnar Myrdal has pointed out, appears to lie in the fact that "the producers, including the employees, all find themselves belonging to clearly distinguished special groups, held together by shared interests, while all are consumers." [35] Producers' interests are easily identifiable, whereas consumers' interests are dispersed. Consequently, when trying collectively to better their socioeconomic conditions, people tend to direct themselves to the producers' aspect: They focus upon increasing their income rather than upon improving the means of spending it. In this latter capacity they continue to act individually even when dealing with gigantic organizations on the producers' side.

Leisure Associations and Mass Media

An important aspect of modernization is the increase of leisure. "Working" and "nonworking" hours tend to become more sharply demarcated, while at the same time the actual number of working hours diminishes. In the Netherlands the development toward a shorter average workday has proceeded a little slower than in most Western industrial societies; this slight retardation seems to be in line with the general lag in modernization apparent in several areas of social and cultural life. Since 1960, a forty-five hour, five-day working week is normal in almost any industry; virtually all wage earners are entitled to an annual vacation of at least two weeks; and for most occupations retirement is fixed at the age of sixty-five.

A great deal of the time now available for leisure is devoted to activities that fit into a national framework. This is the case when people participate in a club belonging to a national federation; it is also the case when they read a magazine or newspaper, listen to the radio, or watch television, for each of these media is a carrier of

national culture. Both the national federations of clubs and the mass media are typical products of modernization. Before the middle of the nineteenth century there were a few national cultural associations and two or three newspapers with a nationwide circulation, but neither reached more than a thin upper layer of society. In 1851, the largest national newspaper printed no more than 5,400 copies.[36] After 1870, however, national associations of many kinds began to proliferate, and the press set out to win subscribers in every social stratum.

Today a vast network of voluntary associations extends throughout Dutch society, providing a wide variety of organized leisure activities. In a nationwide survey in 1955 almost every other adult Dutchman was found to be actively involved in at least one such organization.[37] In size and structure these associations range from large to small, and from ephemeral and informal to strongly established and tightly organized; culturally they cover almost every conceivable field. Except for the very informal ones, most local clubs belong to national federations. Thus in 1963 the Central Bureau of Statistics registered 64 national sports federations, embracing over 17,000 clubs and more than 1,500,000 members.[38]

Among the sports federations, the Royal Dutch Soccer Union ranks first in membership. Its well-documented history exemplifies the rise of the great national leisure associations and brings out several salient aspects of the modernization of Dutch society in general.[39] Soccer was introduced from England in the eighteen seventies. The first local club was founded in 1879, and soon the game spread from one town to another. In 1889, nine clubs came together to establish the Dutch Soccer Union; although the name indicated that this was meant to be a national federation, all the founding clubs had their homes in cities in the western provinces of North and South Holland,

and their members were young men belonging to the well-to-do burgher classes. The next decades brought a fast diffusion, first to the cities in other parts of the country, then after 1900 to the urban working class districts, and finally after 1914 to the rural towns and villages. Typically, the first clubs were all of the "general" nonconfessional type, but soon the Roman Catholics and the Orthodox Protestants followed suit by establishing their own clubs and organizations. In 1940 the three national federations merged into one union; within this union there are still special leagues for the Orthodox Protestants, who play on Saturdays rather than on Sundays.

The development of organized soccer has been hardly less spectacular than the rise of big industry and the trade union movement. In 1910 there were about 100 clubs in the whole country; in 1940, almost 1,000; in 1960, more than 4,000. Membership mounted accordingly, from less than 10,000 in 1910, to over 150,000 in 1940, and to more than 500,000 in 1960. In addition to the registered members there are the interested onlookers and supporters; in 1960 one-third of the male population above the age of twelve went to see a soccer game at least once a month.[40] Membership is always in a local club, but through their club people are involved in a tightly organized national network. Standardized rules govern the game wherever it is played, and the national union sees to it that these rules are observed. Every team, no matter how inept, has its place in a centrally regulated hierarchy of leagues; this classification allows for comparisons on a nationwide scale and draws attention to the top, where the best clubs from all over the country compete for the national championship. The national champions in turn represent the Netherlands in European competitions. These matches, along with the matches of the national shirt team, are avidly followed throughout the country.

Other modern sports have had a similar development, although none of them has become as widely popular as soccer. With but one exception (*korfbal*) they were introduced from abroad, mostly from England, and were first played by small local groups of young men usually belonging to the upper strata. Then came growth and national organization, often accompanied by tendencies toward democratization and *verzuiling*. In the meantime, most traditional sports have declined. There used to be several indigenous Dutch ball games like *kolf*, with many regional and local variations. All of these have receded before the advance of modern sports, with their standardized rules and procedures that make possible national and even international meetings. Insofar as they have survived, the traditional games have taken on a sort of decorative function beside the national standardized sports; cherished for their sentimental and commercial value, they do not any longer belong to the realm of ordinary leisure activities.

The impact of soccer and other modern sports upon Dutch society at large cannot be appraised in isolation from the total impact of modernization. Within this wider context of social and cultural change, soccer has played an unmistakable part, both by directing public interest to the national scene and by promulgating standards of civil behavior appropriate to participants in a larger social structure. It is no accident that soccer was first played by the sons of the bourgeoisie; the game embodies a set of norms akin to those governing the social life of burghers in general. Soccer brings out open rivalry, yet restrains it by rules; it imposes the obligation to meet one's antagonist as one's equal and to respect him regardless of personal feelings. These norms, usually summed up in the notion of "fair play," are not always perfectly internalized; at times they cause great strain both on the fields and in the stands. Yet in the end they are generally vindicated.

Appreciation of this fact no doubt reinforces the tendencies toward civil behavior on the part of players as well as spectators.

As the wider social and cultural functions of soccer became more generally recognized, the Union began to shape its policies toward the deliberate realization of these functions. Today it offers full training programs for youth leaders in order better to exploit the educational possibilities of soccer. Government authorities both on the national and the local levels now support soccer as a positive value in public health as well as social citizenship. At the same time the financial benefits to be reaped from soccer as a spectator game have given rise to professionalism and commercial management. Besides being a pure leisure pursuit, then, soccer is also drawn into the fields of education and welfare and business.

After a long and steady growth, membership in the Soccer Union appears to have reached a plateau during the last few years. Various other leisure organizations are having similar troubles. Similarly, attendance at public sports events, motion pictures, theatrical performances, and concerts has also dropped.[41] Altogether these trends— which, to be sure, are not yet momentous—point toward a "privatization" of leisure: People are tending to appropriate a little more of their free time to individual or family activities and a little less to collective activities. This does not mean, however, that they withdraw from the orbit of national integration. On the contrary, the intermediary contacts of clubs and associations appear to be giving way somewhat to more direct forms of exposure to national communications. For, at the same time that many leisure organizations are facing stagnation and relative decline, the mass media have continued to expand. This holds true of the daily press, which has been increasing its circulation year by year; in certain respects it is also true of the radio; and it is true in a spectacular way of television. Today almost three out of every four households own television sets; in the time budget of the average Dutch family, watching television ranks first among all leisure activities.[42] The impact of television upon the national community has been so great that in 1965 a government had to resign because it failed to settle an issue regarding television.

Together the three media reach practically every Dutch home. In both their organizational structure and cultural content they all bear a markedly national imprint. There are, at this writing, three radio and two television networks, each of which carries its programs into every part of the country. The press offers a greater variety, especially in the way of periodicals, magazines, reviews, and so forth. The number of daily newspapers is growing smaller each year, yet in 1965 it was still no less than eighty-eight.[43]

All Dutch newspapers exhibit some clear common features. None has a very big circulation—the two largest publish just over 300,000 copies. All dailies are sold by subscription; street sales amount to less than 5 per cent. Being delivered directly to the subscriber's home, papers are generally treated as "family papers," and they are edited accordingly. They all apply some commonly accepted standards of decency; thus, they never mention the names or print photographs of defendants in Dutch courts. As a result, by most foreign standards even the most sensational Dutch daily is still moderate in its headlines and discreet in its selection of news.

While generally similar, each Dutch paper is different, presenting a specific selection of items and giving its own commentary. One way in which the papers differ is in the political and confessional sympathies they profess. This obviously bears upon their editorial viewpoint; less obviously perhaps, it sometimes also guides the selection of news so that, for example, the Orthodox Protestant papers never mention any Sunday sports events. Another distinction is between national and provincial or local papers; the former naturally give broader coverage of national and foreign news. A third way in which the papers differ is according to the socioeconomic stratum of their steady readers. Combining these criteria, the Dutch newspapers may be roughly classified as follows:

(a) Two "quality" papers, published in Amsterdam and Rotterdam, both dating from the first half of the nineteenth century, of politically "liberal" sympathies, with a national circulation, mainly among the higher strata, totaling 120,000.

(b) Eight national papers, also published in Amsterdam and Rotterdam, each more or less closely affiliated with a particular political-confessional bloc; readers are concentrated in the medium strata; total circulation close to 1,400,000.

(c) Seventy-eight provincial or local papers, published in all parts of the country, some—especially in the Southern provinces—openly committed to a confessional bloc, but most of them ostensibly neutral; while they cater to all social strata, it is mostly people from the lower strata who read only a paper of this category; total circulation, 2,000,000.

The organizational structure of radio and television is determined by one principle: *verzuiling*. The national government possesses the authority to grant broadcasting licenses, and almost from the beginning in the nineteen twenties, these licenses have been granted exclusively to five, noncommercial corporations representing a "general," a Socialist, a Roman Catholic, an Orthodox Protestant,

and a latitudinarian Protestant segment of the population. Together these corporations share most of the broadcasting time on the radio and television networks, each producing its own programs. Revenue is derived partly from the contributions of individual members (ranging in number from 150,000 to 500,000 per corporation), and partly from license fees on receivers collected by the state.

The immense popularity of television has aroused the interest of business in its possibilities as an advertising medium. The *zuil* corporations have strongly opposed the implied menace to their monopoly. Since the national government disposes of the broadcasting licenses, the fight has been carried into the political arena, where in early 1965, as already noted, it caused a government to resign. Eventually a compromise was arranged, allowing for a modified form of commercial television in which the established corporations can take part, and creating provisions for new applicants to receive broadcasting licenses as well. At the time of this writing, these arrangements have not yet been put into effect, however, so that all broadcasting rights are still reserved to the five *zuil* corporations.

The very idea of *verzuiling* implies a tacit negation of class differences. Consequently, each broadcasting corporation, in an effort to please the taste of the members of all socioeconomic strata, covers the whole range from "highbrow" art to "lowbrow" entertainment. This policy leads to the unintentional consequence that the audience tends to select its programs regardless of the producing corporation. In this way radio and television, while reflecting *verzuiling* in their organizational structure, serve to counteract *verzuiling* in their actual effect.

Two particular events have made this especially clear. The first occurred on November 26–27, 1962, when the "general" broadcasting corporation produced a twenty-four-hour marathon charity drive on both media. Finan-

cially, the drive was a huge success, yielding the unprecedented amount of 18 million guilders ($5 million);
emotionally, it led to an upsurge of national feelings of
solidarity, generosity, and pride. The second memorable
occasion took place on January 4, 1964, when the socialist
corporation broadcasted a satirical program in which
watching television was depicted as a new religion exhibit-
ing familiar texts, symbols, and rituals of Christianity. This
program stirred up a national turmoil that lasted for weeks.
In the general agitation even the wildest negative reac-
tions unwittingly testified to television's efficacy in short-
ening social distances between the various segments of the
Dutch population. Television apparently had confronted
the offended believers with viewpoints to which otherwise
they would never have been exposed.

These were two exceptional occasions, dramatically in-
terrupting the regular day-by-day impact of television
upon Dutch society. Each day television conveys a flow of
information and entertainment to a nationwide audience,
and in both its selection and presentation of items it applies, explicitly or implicitly, a fixed set of values and
norms. In spite of their diverging political and religious
views, the five broadcasting corporations are about equally
committed to the dominant bourgeois culture pattern. Everyone who appears on television professionally conforms
to this pattern in dress, speech, and manners. Thus television strongly reinforces the national model of "civility" in
social behavior.

Verzuiling, Integration, and Conflict

The profusion of national organizations dealing with all
sorts of activities, both compulsory and voluntary, might
not necessarily have resulted in increased integration of
Dutch society as a whole. Clearly, a society may be dis-

rupted rather than integrated when some segments of the population build strong national organizations of their own. In neighboring Belgium, for instance, the competing movements of Flemings and Walloons have caused violent outbreaks of hostility that have jeopardized national unity.

The Netherlands, on the other hand, has hardly ever experienced internal threats to its nationhood. The national structure, established in the late sixteenth and early seventeenth centuries, and for a long time controlled by the burgher elites, has not been assaulted by the popular emancipationist movements of the past hundred years. Instead of opposing the national structure as such, the formerly excluded minorities have claimed an equitable share in it, seeking integration according to the typical pattern of *verzuiling*.

For some generations *verzuiling*, based upon the two dimensions of religious and socioeconomic differences, has more or less monopolized all expressions of organized conflict in Dutch society. No other social division has yielded any lasting preponderant issues. Modernization has brought formerly distant geographical regions into closer contact, thus enhancing the possibilities of either conflict or integration. In effect, integration has outweighed conflict by far; the few conflicts that do arise do not usually concern interregional friction but express mostly protests against alleged regional neglect or injury suffered from the national community. Other conceivable sources of discord between various social segments have also failed to bring about nationwide alignments. Female subordination, at one time the focus of a fervent emancipationist movement, has not quite disappeared, but it has ceased to be a major issue in Dutch society. Nor do age differences engender large-scale ruptures. There is a union of pensioners acting as a national pressure group, and there are occasional local clashes between teen-agers and the police, but neither the lawful actions of the aged nor the provocative exploits of the young become matters of great national significance.

Religious and socioeconomic issues, then, are the principal foci of national conflict in Dutch society. Neither, however, presents a clear-cut dichotomy like the Flemish-Walloon antithesis in Belgium. As it was pointed out in Chapter III, the Dutch population is divided on the basis of religious confession into four major social categories: the two sharply demarcated blocs of the Roman Catholics and the orthodox Calvinists or *Gereformeerden,* on the one hand, and the two more vaguely outlined congeries of the latitudinarian Protestants and the "unchurchly" on the other. We have also shown that socioeconomic status may be defined by at least five different criteria: economic function, size of income, source of income, kind of work, and occupational prestige—each criterion yielding a specific classification. Given this multiform differentiation of the population, it is understandable that the two dividing principles of religious and socioeconomic identification have not produced a single cleavage splitting the nation into radically opposed camps.

From the beginning, the cardinal goal of the confessional organizations has been to keep together the believers of all social strata. The Roman Catholic People's Union, founded in 1881, was intended "to reconcile the various walks of life" by shielding the workers and tradesmen against "the social errors of our time." [44] This program implied a stand against the doctrines of liberalism and, in particular, socialism—a position that has been modified but never abandoned. In 1954 the Dutch Bishops issued a pastoral letter forbidding all Roman Catholics to join a socialist trade union, to visit socialist meetings, to read socialist newspapers, or to listen to socialist radio programs, on penalty of exclusion from the holy sacraments

—the severest sanction for a true believer. Unfortunately, the impact of this episcopal decree has never been investigated. It does not appear to have retrieved many of those who had already committed themselves to frequent socialist contacts. As far as radio listening is concerned, the decree certainly has not been carried out to the letter, but in other respects its effects may have been stronger. In any case, it has drawn a sharp line between Roman Catholicism and socialism, and it may have withheld many from taking the decisive step of crossing that line. In 1965 the ban upon socialist unions was revoked; the other strictures are still standing but seem to be largely inoperative today.

The *Gereformeerden,* divided over several churches, do not have an ecclesiastical hierarchy comparable to that of the Roman Catholics. Yet they too have succeeded in building strong national organizations covering almost every field and spanning all socioeconomic divisions. Even more than the Roman Catholics, however, the *Gereformeerden* have always tended to resign themselves to being a minority. Following the device of one of their nineteenth-century leaders, they have sought "strength in isolation"; this position has been given ideological support in an elaborate doctrine of subcultural sovereignty.[45] From their firmly organized entrenchments both the Roman Catholics and the *Gereformeerden* continue to press their respective claims upon the national community; but even if these claims are met only halfway or not at all, both blocs keep their allegiance to the national status quo.

One specific factor furthering this compliance may be the scattered geographical distribution of the religious confessions. As indicated above, there are some strong regional concentrations of Roman Catholics as well as *Gereformeerden.* The southern provinces of North Brabant and Limburg have to a large extent an homogeneous Roman Catholic population; yet more Roman Catholics live in all other parts of the country combined. The *Gereformeerden* find themselves in a similar situation: In spite of regional clusters, the majority lives scattered about the country. This dispersion, preventing allegiances from gravitating to distinct territorial units, has probably been conducive to the process of integration within the established national structure.

The final aim of the confessional blocs can perhaps be described best as "segmented integration": they aspire to participate in all national decision-making and to benefit fully from all national facilities while at the same time maintaining internal unity and cohesion. In practice this means that they are willing to collaborate with others at the level of leadership, while at the same time trying to keep their rank and file insulated. In the preceding sections we have come across several instances where the confessional blocs proved to be more "open at the top" and "closed at the bottom." These correspond to a general tendency inherent in *verzuiling,* a tendency that is revealingly expressed in the image of separate pillars supporting a common roof.

In its neat simplicity the image may also suggest too much order, however. Actually the situation is highly entangled, if only because not all *zuilen* are based upon the same distinguishing criteria. Whereas the confessional blocs find their uniting principle in religion, the secular blocs deny the general validity of this very principle in social organization. The latter stress specific socioeconomic views and interests, both distinctions that the confessional blocs try to neutralize.

The contingency of these two divergent axes renders the whole system of *verzuiling* very complex. Even the very number of *zuilen* may be made a matter of discussion. Some observers count only three: the Roman Catholic, the orthodox Calvinist, and the "neutral" *zuil*. They thus ignore the second dimension of *verzuiling*, which is no less essential to a proper understanding of its actual dynamics. It seems clearer, therefore, to make a systematic distinction between the so-called "general" or "liberal" bloc as opposed to the socialist bloc. The boundaries, to be sure, are vague and fluid, and in some areas, such as school education, they are virtually absent; yet wherever they become manifest they prove to be quite trenchant, as in politics, where the Liberal and the Socialist parties represent two sharply opposed poles. In principle both the Liberals and the Socialists reject *verzuiling;* yet in practice they are forced to accept it, and to assume themselves the role of *zuilen* in the shifting coalitions with the two confessional blocs.

The same situation holds for the large socioeconomic organizations. They, too, have to operate in a field subdivided by lines of religious confession and of liberalism and socialism. The economy generates a wide range of opposing interests such as between the rich and the poor, the farmers and the industrialists, the wage earners and the pensioners, the employers and the employees, the white collar and the blue collar workers, and the producers and the consumers. As these potential conflicts give rise to national organizations, they tend to be drawn into the pattern of *verzuiling*. The religious blocs do not wish socioeconomic issues to detract from loyalty to the confessional formation; they therefore provide organizations incorporating these issues. By doing so, however, they also allow an element of internal tension to enter their ranks.

Thus the two crossing axes in the system of *verzuiling* are continuously at odds. Socioeconomic antagonisms threaten to upset the confessional blocs, while confessional differences disturb the unity of socioeconomic categories. By thus confounding the issues and dividing the loyalties, *verzuiling* probably adds to the stability of the national order.[46]

National unity and stability are further promoted, so it seems, since the leaders of all *zuilen* unite, in spite of their diverging world views, in accepting an ethic of civility and orderliness. Civility, in its most "ideal" and perfectly internalized form, includes not only good manners and a sense of decorum but also more personal qualities such as self-possession and a sense of duty and responsibility. Anyone holding or aspiring to a leading position in Dutch society, whether in government, politics, business, or any other organizational area, has to acknowledge these standards. They have the effect of imbuing all conflict with some restraint, and of minimizing open outbursts of enmity.

These tendencies are reinforced by the time-honored tradition of orderliness in Dutch society, a tradition that proceeds from its international power position and the unmilitaristic proclivities of its burgher elite. For the past twenty years the ethic of orderliness has dominated the field of industrial relations in particular.[47] On the whole it has provided a suitable climate for the intricately balanced relationships at the national level of *verzuiling*.

But the whole system is in continual flux. The very word *verzuiling* (pillarization) indicates a process and not a static condition. Historically, as we have seen, *verzuiling* can be understood as the step-by-step introduction of three popular emancipationist movements into a national structure that used to be dominated by the conservative-liberal bourgeoisie. To a large extent this process of integration has been successful. The leaders of the respective blocs now accept each other as equal partners in the national community. The blurring of once insurmountable distinctions is nicely demonstrated by the career of Willem

Drees, prime minister during the years 1948 to 1958; a man of middle-class origins, he achieved the highest possible position in the Dutch state as a member of the Socialist Labor party; in the successive governments he presided over, every *zuil* was represented at least once.

It may well be that the process of *verzuiling* has already reached its pinnacle and is now on the decline.[48] In some areas, especially education, the confessional blocs are still gaining strength; in others, such as organized sports, they appear to be losing ground. By and large it is plausible to expect that the integration accomplished at the top will gradually descend to the lower levels as well.[49] Several factors possibly favoring such a development may be mentioned. One is that increasing prosperity and leisure widen people's range of orientation, enabling them to make comparisons with other creeds and other social strata. Most effective in this broadening process is the impact of radio and television. The mass media and the schools also stimulate the general diffusion of the elitist standards of civility, facilitating "intersegmental" relationships. Closely related to each of these trends is the general "erosion of the religious landscape," [50] expressed both in increasing secularization and religious apostasy and in the ecumenical rapprochement between different churches.

Some American sociologists have discerned signs of American society moving in the direction of a form of denominational segmentation similar to the Dutch.[51] We shall not enter into the merits of their arguments with regard to the United States. As far as the Netherlands is concerned, however, the opposite prospect of a gradual "depillarization" of society seems more likely. This conjecture, to be sure, speculates upon a far distant future; at the moment the *zuilen* still stand solidly, dominating the national scene.

{V}

Family
and
Community

The Family

The vast majority of Dutchmen, young and old, live in families. Less than 10 per cent live alone or in larger institutions, and for most of these, this is only a temporary stage. One is born into a family, spends the first years of life almost exclusively within it, then develops further-reaching relationships, until eventually, as an adult, one leaves one's family of origin in order to found a new family of one's own, thus continuing the cycle.

In this chapter we shall use the word "family" to refer to the nuclear family, the small conjugal unit of husband, wife, and children. As in all Western European societies, in the Netherlands the nuclear family is today the basic unit of residence and kinship. The Dutch language is felicitous in providing a special word: *gezin*, which denotes both the aspect of matrimony and parenthood and the state of dwelling together. Because of this latter condition a person can be a member of one *gezin* only; leaving the parental home at marriage inevitably entails leaving the parental *gezin*.

All wider kinship relations center around the *gezin*. They are wholly bilateral: Husband and wife have to treat relatives by birth or by marriage as equally near, and for the children no formal distinctions exist between father's kin and mother's kin. As a result, kinship relationships are typically open; instead of closed clans held together by a common lineage, one finds an almost endless range of links through which individual nuclear families are reciprocally related. Within this wide range it is only the first-degree relationships that really count, that is, the relationships linking the members of one nuclear family (in an ascendant line) to the members of the parents' "families of orientation," and (in a descendent line) to the members of the children's "families of procreation." In this whole system the emphasis is obviously upon the nuclear family as the basic unit.[1]

The family, while being of great import in shaping the lives of its members, is by no means autonomous. As a microsocial unit it is subject to macrosocial forces in at least three interrelated ways. First, the family is subject to national laws and norms, some, the marriage contract for example, strictly formal, others, such as the standards of proper household management, less precise but nonetheless compelling. Second, the family is involved in long-range macrosocial trends: industrialization, mechanization, urbanization, democratization, and various other modernizing processes. Third, families reflect the differences created by macrosocial divisions, such as age, residence, socioeconomic stratum, and religion. Thus, the main themes treated in the previous chapters—the histori-

cal perspective, the lines of differentiation, and the forces
of national integration—recur as pertinent factors in the
Dutch family.

First of all, the variety of family styles should be noted.
The "typical Dutch family" exists no more than does the
"typical Dutchman." Age, to begin with, makes for many
differences. It marks successive stages of size and affluence
through which a family passes; in addition, it fixes the
family's position in the sequence of generations differently
affected by modernization. Residence is also a notable
differentiating factor. Although regional distinctions are
diminishing, they sometimes prove to be quite resistant,
especially within the family sphere. Rural-urban contrasts
grow smaller, too; yet while rural families increasingly
take the urban family as a model, the conditions of rural
life continue to qualify rural family styles.[2]

Residence is still a most important variable in combination with another one, socioeconomic class. Unfortunately, little research has been done on the relations between family and class in Dutch society. Rural family life
has been studied extensively but with rather small emphasis upon class variables. Investigations into the urban family have been confined mainly to the lower classes. Only
one study, by a foreign observer, has been published on
the urban middle-class family; this study, moreover, is of
limited validity.[3] Lower-class homes are apparently more
accessible to social research. Yet even here interest has
tended to be one-sided, since several investigations were
sponsored by social work agencies with a particular concern for "problem" families. Consequently, we seem to be
better informed on lower-class "problem" families than on
"normal" families.

But in spite of the scarcity of research, some distinctions
between middle-class and lower-class families stand out
clearly enough. First of all, the divergent material condi-

tions of the homes cannot escape notice. Lower-class houses are smaller and more crowded and less well-equipped with modern amenities. The housing shortage, generally considered a major national problem, is felt most acutely among young families in the lower income brackets. They often have to live with parental families for a number of years before being allotted houses of their own. For those couples who possess the means for paying a higher rent or buying a house, the shortage is far less pressing.[4]

Besides material conditions, the cultural climate also differs between socioeconomic strata. The topics and modes of conversation, the kind of language used, the prevailing ideas and opinions, the ways of household management, and the methods of education are all to a considerable degree classbound. The precise meaning and extent of these cultural distinctions have not been studied in any detail, yet their over-all significance is evident.

The importance of the family as a carrier of cultural differences has been demonstrated most clearly in the area of religion. As pointed out in Chapter III, most Dutch families are religiously homogeneous, with husband, wife, and children embracing the same creed. This is true in particular of Roman Catholic and *Gereformeerde* families, both of which also show the most distinctive denominational identity. Many family activities in Roman Catholic or *Gereformeerde* homes are attended with religious symbols and rituals.[5] A child born into a family where faith figures so prominently is raised as a matter of course in the appropriate religious spirit, and will usually, again as a matter of course, marry a spouse of the same creed. Thus, families transmit religious differences from one generation to the next.

Overruling all differences associated with age, residence, class, and creed, however, are some common na-

tional standards incumbent upon all families. According
to the law as well as to generally accepted morality, the
family must be based upon marriage. Marriage must be
monogamous; it cannot be concluded by close relatives;
minors need special consent. By law, marriage is a civil
contract; although in about two-thirds of the cases the
civil ceremony is followed by a church wedding, the latter
has no legal validity. The marital state entails several specific rights and obligations, entitling the husband to the
status of "head of the family," committing both spouses to
mutual fidelity, and conferring upon them a joint responsibility for their children. The marital union may not be
broken freely at the partners' wish; divorce is possible only
on specific terms and after protracted legal proceedings,
the four recognized reasons being adultery, willful deser-
tion, long-term prison sentence, and grave physical mal-
treatment. Apart from marriage, other aspects of family
life are also subject to state legislation. Thus children
must be properly reared and sent to school in time; the
household economy must be orderly managed; minimum
standards of hygiene must be fulfilled. If a family fails to
meet any of these standards, the state is apt to interfere
by means of social work agencies or penal courts.

Besides being subject to fixed legal arrangements, all
Dutch families find themselves involved in the general
process of modernization. Modernization, to be sure, is not
a neatly synchronized development reaching all families at
once and to the same degree. Different milieux are passing
through different stages of modernization and are undergoing these stages in different ways. Yet, in spite of the
manifold variations, it is possible to discern some systematic tendencies, which will be discussed in the following
paragraphs. It should be understood, however, that these
observations are of a very general nature and can be ap-

plied to any specific type of family only after due qualifications.

The most conspicuous long-range trend, clearly evident in the statistical records, is the *decreasing size of the family*. The average number of persons per household was 4.82 in 1899, dropped to 4.64 in 1920, 4.01 in 1947, 3.86 in 1960, and to 3.76 in 1964.[6] The immediate causes of this decrease are twofold. In the first place, the number of children per family has diminished steadily: while the gross average for all families in the 1899 census was 2.47, this had dropped to 1.80 in 1960. In the second place, the number of persons not belonging to the actual nuclear family but living with it as members of the *gezin* has shown an even greater decline: from 0.30 in 1920 to 0.24 in 1930, 0.16 in 1947, and 0.15 in 1960. Both tendencies are the outcome of other more basic trends affecting the family.

One such trend is the *separation of the family from kinship and community*, a process known by various names, such as "individualization" or the transition from an "open" to a "closed" family type. The "open" family lived literally with open, unlocked doors through which relatives and neighbors could freely enter. In the countryside and in the old urban working-class districts this open family type has prevailed for a long time, and in many communities it still exists. The burgher city elites, on the other hand, have always tended to favor "closed" family living; they preferred the privacy secured by carefully demarcating their domicile. Today this pattern is rapidly becoming the standard to which most families aspire: The conjugal family should live a life of its own, in a separate house with an independent income, enjoying a proper measure of privacy and autonomy. When the housing shortage forces a newlywed couple to move in with a parental family, this is regarded as prompted by emergency and is viewed as an infringement upon the norm that each family should have its own home. Often great pains are taken to keep the two households apart.

The individualization of the family does not imply the severance of all larger kinship ties. Rather, as so often is the case in social change, this trend represents a modification rather than the total breakup of existing conditions. Many kinship contacts remain, such as mutual visits, exchange of gifts, and aid in case of need. Most of these contacts are limited to first-degree relatives, however. They are, furthermore, dependent upon physical proximity; migration greatly intensifies the isolation and individualization of the family. In addition, the greater social and economic security provided by a regular wage or salary and backed by welfare legislation lessens the need to rely upon relatives and neighbors.

The economic functions of the family have altered considerably. It is sometimes said that the family has altogether changed from a productive into a consumptive unit. This seems to be rather overstressing the point; the significant shift is the *segregation of family and occupation.* Surely no single family today can be economically self-sufficient, but neither can any family afford to be altogether unproductive. "Production" is a tricky concept; yet there can be no doubt as to the positive economic value of many household tasks such as cooking, repairing, and maintenance of family possessions. Of principal importance, however, is the fact that the results of these activities remain within the family as fruits of leisure, and they are not assessed as income. Actual income, on the other hand, derives from sources outside the family, usually from a job performed by the husband, sometimes from pensions or capital interests. In contrast to the older types of family farming or home industry, where all family members participated in a common economic pursuit, the household as such now stands apart from the occupational world where work is remunerated with money.

As a corollary to this shift in economic function, the family is becoming increasingly important as a *center of leisure*. Surveys have shown that more than 60 per cent of the time available for leisure is spent at home and that at least 75 per cent of the free time spent outside the home is passed in the company of members of the family.[7] These figures are averages for the whole population. If we leave out the age categories between fifteen and twenty-five, which are least inclined to family activities, the percentages are even higher. Interestingly, with ascending age, as family life takes up an increasing portion of leisure, the amount of time allotted to friendships diminishes. For most people between thirty and fifty the family is the predominant if not the exclusive domain of leisure.[8] Accordingly, several modern leisure institutions are typically geared to participation by families. This applies most clearly to vacations, but also in everyday life, the married couple is more or less the standard unit for social evening calls or for visits to concert and theater. Clearly, the growing monopolization of leisure by the family is related to the separation from kinship and community as well as to the segregation of household and occupation. The joint implications are far-reaching. The occupational world puts increasingly heavy demands upon people's capacities for civility and self-restraint. The family, providing a niche where one can find intimacy and privacy and where one can be "oneself," thus gains importance as a refuge for the expression of emotions and affective feelings. This tendency is related in turn to a growing popularity of the ideal of romantic love and to greater freedom of courtship and mate selection.

Various statistical trends bear witness to the mounting

importance of the affective functions of the family. One such trend is the rising percentage of married persons in the population. While in 1920, 16.2 per cent of all women of the ages 40 to 44 were unmarried, this percentage had decreased to 10.1 in 1960; at the same time the average age at first marriage has dropped steadily. It seems plausible to interpret these figures to the effect that marriage and family life tend to become more universal as society provides fewer alternatives for intimacy and free display of emotions. The greater affective demands made upon family life may also be gathered from what might seem contrary evidence: the percentage of marriages dissolved by divorce, a percentage that increased from 0.66 in 1899 to 2.19 in 1957, in spite of tightened legal restrictions.[9] Figures of quite another kind, the suicide rates, may also testify to the emotional significance of the family; in 1963 the official suicide rate was 9.5 per 100,000 citizens; the subdivisions as to marital state were 7.4 for the married, 8.9 for the unmarried, 38.2 for the divorced, and 28.2 for the widowed. Finally, as a fourth statistical testimony to the increased emphasis on affection in the family, we may point to the slowly descending birth rate. The reproductive duties of the family recede for the pleasures of companionship and sexual partnership; family planning also signifies the shift away from obedience to traditional authorities toward autonomous determination.

Closely related to, and partly implied in, the changes mentioned so far is the tendency toward *greater egalitarianism within the family*. Again, this means that long-established inequalities are being modified, not that they have altogether ceased to exist. In the average Dutch family the father is still the "head," not merely *de jure* but also *de facto*. However, his authority is not as undivided and as undisputed as it used to be. The old patriarchal system with the father ruling the extended family can still be found in some rural regions, but it is definitely on the wane. The segregation of family and occupation has deprived the husband of his role as household chief; the separation from the larger kinship network and the increasing importance of affective ties have also furthered equal companionship between the spouses. The precise extent of these changes is impossible to assess; it seems that many men profess equality more readily than they practice it. The scanty evidence we possess, nonetheless, does suggest that in more "modern" families the husband participates more often in domestic tasks, while the wife has a stronger voice in important family decisions.[10] Still, as pointed out in Chapter III, the dominant norm decrees that women should primarily be occupied with domestic tasks; the percentage of married women in the labor force is still remarkably low.

Parent-child relations also seem to be altering toward greater egalitarianism. Here research findings are completely lacking, so we can only suggest some likely analogies with the general trend as revealed in other modern Western societies. As is the case elsewhere, change and mobility are liable to affect parental authority; the schools and the mass media, in taking over a considerable part of education, also probably detract a due share of prestige and influence from the parents. In all likelihood these tendencies are as pronounced in Dutch society as in other modern societies, but no specific evidence is available.

Recognition of the various modernizing processes finally raises the question of whether or not the Dutch family still possesses any typically Dutch features. This is a precarious question; the simplest answer would be to repeat that *the* Dutch family does not exist. This, however, seems too easy a way out. After all, there is a common stereotype that the family in the Netherlands plays a more prominent role in social life than in neighboring countries. This stereotype, moreover, can be supported by some official figures: for example, there are fewer cafés in the Netherlands and people go less often to the cinema.[11] Such figures reinforce the generally shared impression that the Dutch seek comfort first of all in the family, that they cherish the private rather than the public sphere.

For the past two centuries Dutch writers have shown an intense preoccupation with the family. The "family novel" has developed into a literary genre of its own. One should read, as a good example, *Old People and the Things That Pass* by Louis Couperus,[12] which dramatically describes the introverted family life among the burgher aristocracy of The Hague around 1900. The author, for the sake of literary structure, has perhaps depicted the family relationships as even more exclusive than in fact they were; but even so he seems to have indicated something essential of the enclosing privacy of the family in the solid Dutch burgher milieu.

Women in particular were enveloped in the bourgeois family. Within the narrowly confined domestic circle, they cultivated the virtues of primness and neatness and the pleasures of homely coziness or *gezelligheid*. The example thus set by the leading burgher families has become the guiding model for Dutch family life in every stratum. Just as in the older cities the houses in the side streets are smaller replicas of the burgher mansions along the main canals, so the dominant family style has also spread from *grande bourgeoisie* to *petite bourgeoisie*. Great value is attached to family cohesion; birthdays and wedding anniversaries are regularly observed. The most striking manifestation of family culture takes place on December 5, when the Saint Nicholas feast seals the unity of each family with gifts and homemade poetry; almost every family celebrates this annual occasion.

Dutch family culture has not been studied sufficiently

to allow for a sound comparative assessment. The observations made above are predominantly impressionistic and to a large extent guided by common lore. But it is plausible that two typically Dutch features, the burgher inheritance and the tenacity of religious divisions, are connected with the strongly introverted family culture. Privacy, concern for respectability, orderliness, discretion, seclusiveness—in all such traits the traditions of burgherdom and *verzuiling* seem to converge with the prevailing family style. If there are any distinct Dutch national character traits, these are likely to be nourished in the family.

Communities

In the process of modernization spatial boundaries become less important in shaping social and cultural life. Modern means of transport and communication have mitigated people's dependency upon the immediate environment and widened the range of social contacts and cultural orientations. As a result, the local community is no longer an inclusive social context enveloping the lives of its members from birth to death.

Yet locality continues to be an essential element in the formal as well as the informal structure of society. Formally the Dutch state is subdivided into eleven provinces and over 950 municipalities. The municipalities, although slightly less autonomous than their counterparts in the United States,[13] maintain a considerable degree of independent authority in local matters regarding schools, housing, public health, and so forth. To many citizens the town hall is still the most concrete manifestation of public authority. Politically the municipalities also continue to carry weight. Town board elections, apart from their intrinsic local interest, may serve as significant indicators of political developments; participation in local government can be a useful training ground for political action and a stepping-stone to national politics.

The municipalities vary greatly in size. There are no huge metropolitan conglomerations; the largest municipality, Amsterdam, has 870,000 inhabitants, and according to many planners and politicians, it should not become larger. On the other hand, there are still almost a hundred municipalities with fewer than 1,000 inhabitants; many of these have been separate political units since the Middle Ages. In order to curtail the autonomy the cities had enjoyed during the Republic, equal legal powers were given in the early nineteenth century to all municipalities, large and small. Today, the small municipalities are by and large poorly equipped to fulfill the differentiated tasks of modern administration. A program of amalgamations has therefore been drafted, and it is slowly being put into effect, often against tense local resistance. Between 1950 and 1964, the total number of municipalities dropped from 1,014 to 967.

Besides the political organization of towns and villages into municipalities, Dutch society has known of old another kind of communal organization, the water boards.[14] The fact that a great part of the country is only inhabitable by virtue of continuous and systematic water control has always constituted an incentive to common local effort: Only a community could build and maintain the dikes and windmills required to avert the constant threat of inundation. Thus, from the early Middle Ages each district in the lowlands had its own water board, composed of local people charged with the protection of the land from lakes and sea and invested with the power to levy contributions in labor and money. Several writers have suggested that this early form of communal cooperation has inculcated a sense of democracy in the Dutch people. Even more plausible, although similarly impossible to verify, is the assumption that the organized defense against the sea has enhanced communal solidarity. The local water boards have left their mark on the history of Dutch water control; problems of drainage were often approached in a narrowly parochial fashion, and demands for contributions to more encompassing regional constructions met regularly with all sorts of local chicaneries. In the long run, larger bodies have gradually taken over the main tasks and powers of the local boards. Today a national governmental department possesses full authority in all matters regarding water control; it supervises such projects as the draining of the Zuiderzee and the closing of several big estuaries in South Holland and Zeeland. In accordance with an old Dutch tradition, it combines these tasks with the management of bridges and highways. Meanwhile the local water boards still continue to engage all landowners in the communal implementation of water control. They do not any longer embrace the whole population, however; in urban areas today most people are hardly aware of their existence.

A highly important factor in the formal organization of Dutch communities has been the church. Most municipalities originated as parishes and acquired a distinct administrative status only after the ecclesiastical boundaries had been drawn. The Reformation, while establishing religious diversity in the Netherlands as a whole, did not always impair the religious homogeneity of local areas: More often than not, a whole congregation either was converted to Protestantism or remained Roman Catholic. In the communities where unity of faith was preserved, the church maintained a strong integrative function. It attended all crucial events in a person's life with communal ceremony: birth, wedding, and death were accompanied by religious *rites de passage* at which the whole congregation assembled. Culturally, the church provided the bond

of one belief for all; socially, it united the whole community in the weekly service. In Roman Catholic parishes
common acceptance of ritual and doctrine bestowed a
sense of fellowship on all members; in Protestant congre-
gations the lay duties of church administration stimulated
active communal participation.

In spite of increased social mobility and encroaching
secularization, many towns and villages have remained religiously homogeneous. Local unity of faith is usually reflected in political life and, consequently, in municipal
government. Thus many Roman Catholic municipalities
in the southern provinces have local ordinances forbidding
such varied activities as the sale of contraceptives or mixed
swimming of men and women in public swimming pools.
Several staunchly Calvinist villages in the northern parts
have similarly "puritan" municipal legislation.

The majority of Dutch municipalities today have a
varied religious composition. This includes all large cities
and many medium-sized and small towns as well. Wherever religious diversity prevails, local conditions are
marked by *verzuiling*. Both formal and informal contacts
are to a large extent guided by religious divisions. Not only
are there different churches, but each denomination also
tends to have its own schools, community centers, and
health facilities. The duplication or triplication of local
services may lead to economic waste; in small towns it
sometimes results in a virtual void: For want of cooperation, very little can be accomplished.

The pattern of community *verzuiling* often receives
strong support from outside agencies. Thus the national
government has deliberately organized the colonization of
the newly reclaimed Zuiderzee *polders* in such a way that
each village contains an appropriate mixture of Roman
Catholics, Dutch Reformed, *Gereformeerden,* and the
"unchurchly." Separate churches have been built for each

denomination, and segregated schools, health organizations, farmers unions, and leisure associations have been founded. The settlers do not seem to have objected to this planned pattern of *verzuiling*.[15] Some evidence has been collected in older rural communities, however, suggesting that *verzuiling* may be regretted and sometimes even resented by the ordinary villagers as something imposed from above. Thus in a village in Drente the local leaders, backed by provincial and national organizations, appeared to be far more keen about denominationally "pure" community services than were the majority of common parishioners.[16]

Verzuiling accentuates the potentially disruptive effect upon community life that is inherent in formal organization. On the one hand, local formal organizations may reinforce communal cohesion by providing a common meeting-ground and a focus of community identification. On the other hand, they may also stress particular interests to the exclusion of the more diffuse communal bonds. Recently the trend has been by and large in the latter direction of functional segmentation. As Ernst Abma concludes in a study on community health services: "Villagers no longer meet and do things together as members of the village community but as members of one or other of the special interest associations or in their occupational pursuits." [17]

As in all Western societies, modernization has thoroughly upset the local community as a cohesive group encompassing the total round of life. In the nineteenth century many villages still approached the ideal type of the communal "folk society": small, isolated, homogeneous, stable, and traditional. Vestiges of the old community culture persist in many rural regions, but always mixed with modern elements. When the American anthropologists John and Dorothy Keur visited the village of Anderen in

Drente in 1952, they noted precisely this blend of tradi-
tionalism and modernity. The life cycle of the villagers
still evolved mostly within definite local boundaries, and
behavior continued to be guided to a large extent by custom. Communal feelings were strong: from birth on children were "gently indoctrinated not so much as individuals, but as members of a group." [18] Yet at the same time
the authors noted a gradual but irretrievable breakdown
of village isolation, evinced in increased economic dependence as well as in a greater sensitivity to outside
standards.

The tension prevailing in many rural areas between
traditional communal autonomy and the leveling impact
of modernization has been highlighted at times in recent
years by the occurrence of incidents of *volksgericht* or
popular justice.[19] In many villages a breach of the norms,
such as committing adultery or jilting a pregnant girl,
would traditionally bring forth communal sanctions by
which the culprits were put to public shame in a rough
and ready manner. These cases of a community taking the
law into its own hands have become increasingly rare. If
such an incident occurs nowadays, it will almost inevitably be reported in the press, arousing national outcry
and derision. Thus the community will find itself exposed
to treatment similar to that it had given its own victim but
on a far larger scale.

Not only do villagers more and more orient themselves
toward outside standards, but many of them leave the village. In some parts of the country, especially in Groningen, Friesland, and Zeeland, the "rural exodus" has been a
familiar movement for quite some time. The small settlements fail to meet the rising demands of the inhabitants;
once people begin to move away, local provisions are apt
to deteriorate so that eventually the community may be
left with few, if any, services of its own. It is not unlikely

that the generally prevailing housing shortage has curbed the tendency toward departure. In many rural areas where agriculture no longer provides sufficient employment, instead of moving away, people have turned to commuting to nearby industrial centers.[20]

Vestiges of traditional community life persist not only in villages but also in some old urban working-class quarters. People in these neighborhoods are often highly aware of their communal identity. The physical boundaries have a real meaning to them; beyond these boundaries they do not feel at home. The community as such is held together by adjoining neighborhoods and by a complex of interlocking family relationships. A similar pattern of matrilineal kinship ties that Michael Young and Peter Willmott encountered in East London has also been found in the old city quarters of Amsterdam and Rotterdam.[21] Here too, however, multifarious renovations are changing both the physical milieu and the social and cultural climate. New families are moving in, often secluding themselves from obtrusive neighborly contacts. Older families are moving out in even greater numbers, some voluntarily, attracted by better jobs and dwellings elsewhere, others forced by municipal housing laws and zoning policies.

An increasingly large part of the population finds itself living in modern town and city developments, set up according to officially planned architectural arrangements and following a more or less uniform style throughout the country. The new dwelling areas, although varied in size and affluence, exhibit some common characteristics. The segregation of family and occupation is almost complete—the husbands leave in the morning and return in the evening. The age structure tends to be skewed, reflecting the predominance of young families as first settlers. The inhabitants are of mixed geographical origin, and many of them keep in touch with relatives and friends in their former place of residence. As a rule people live on friendly terms with their neighbors, but there is no vigorous community spirit.

More or less the same suburban trends are manifest in all modern societies. One typical Dutch feature seems to be the continued absence, so far, of huge metropolitan conglomerations. From the very beginning, urbanism in the Netherlands has developed in a string of competing cities and towns and not in one dominating center. Amsterdam, while being the *primus inter pares,* and worthy of the name capital, has not outstripped its rivals in the fashion of most other European capitals. The Hague has always remained the seat of government and the administrative center, Rotterdam has become the leading port, and even Utrecht owes to its central location a prominent national function. Thus the Netherlands, the most densely populated country of Europe, has no huge metropolis. Recently the term *Randstad* Holland ("Rim City") has found general acceptance to indicate the high degree of urban growth in a ring of cities in the western provinces. This whole *Randstad,* however, is smaller in size and population, and less densely populated, than London or New York. Within the *Randstad* the main agglomerations are still clearly demarcated, physically as well as socially and culturally, as separate urban units.

Meanwhile mobility and traffic between the various cities are increasing steadily. In 1947, 11.5 per cent of the labor force commuted daily to another municipality; by 1960 the number had mounted to 18.3 per cent. The average distances covered are small in terms both of mileage and time when compared with New York, for example. Accordingly, the bicycle and the small motor bike are still the most popular means of transportation for the journey to work, used by no less than 50 per cent of all commuters; only 40 per cent commute by public transport, and 10 per cent by car. The use of automobiles, however, is steadily expanding.[22] The prosperity of the early sixties has also brought forth a burgeoning tendency for people to have two dwellings, one in town and another one in the country for weekends and vacations. This form of split residence symbolizes perhaps best of all the dwindling importance of the community as the all-inclusive social matrix.

Yet, although the modern residential area does not form a community in the traditional sense, it still has a definite social meaning. The segregation of family and occupation allows to the men as breadwinners only limited opportunities for community participation. On the other hand, the wives, the children, and, if present, the elderly, spend most of the day within the local area; they therefore still rely largely upon neighborly contact for their social relationships.[23] Locality, furthermore, has a very effective function in articulating and prolongating class distinctions. For most people, address continues to be an important indicator of social status. Especially in the large cities the dwelling areas of different income groups are situated at considerable distances. Since residence strongly determines the social environment in which the children play and go to school, the physical segregation of the various districts furthers the continuation of cultural differences between socioeconomic classes.

{VI}

Conclusion

Two familiar themes have guided our discussion of Dutch society: continuity and change on the one hand, and unity and diversity on the other. The historically-oriented Chapter II focuses on continuity and change; it shows how certain present features of Dutch society can be traced back to the late sixteenth century and how Dutch social structure and culture are exposed to various modernizing forces. Chapter III on differentiation outlines the diversity of the Dutch population by age, sex, residence, creed, and socioeconomic status. The theme of unity is taken up in Chapter IV on national integration. In Chapter V, the two pairs of concepts are used to describe some aspects of the family and the local community.

The continuity of Dutch society has been remarkable. Within the boundaries set by the state, a distinctive society has persisted for more than three centuries. Major internal upheavals have been few. The intervening periods of foreign occupation—by the French in 1795–1813, by the Germans in 1940–1945[1]—have only strengthened national cohesion. Several features have marked Dutch society throughout its history. From the beginning the country has shown a great variety of distinctive regions; among these regions the maritime western provinces have always predominated. Burghers have formed the traditional elite in Dutch society; their cultural influence is still great. Continuity is also expressed in the perpetuating lines of religious division and in the singular way in which these religious divisions color practically every aspect of social structure and culture.

Continuity does not necessarily imply absence of change; in the Netherlands the two have usually proved quite compatible. The advent of modernization has not radically ended the mainstream of Dutch national traditions; rather, these traditions have bent to flow into more "modern" currents. The modernization of Dutch society, as has been stressed, can be understood as a process of acculturation to a rapidly changing world environment. The responses to modernity have been varied; some modern ways have found eager acceptance by virtually the whole population, others have met with strong resistance in certain sectors.[2] The relatively slow decline of the Dutch birth rate, for example, testifies to a widespread resistance to particular aspects of modernization. Foreign inventions have largely determined the direction of change in recent times, and the actual rate of change has also been directly influenced by international tendencies. In the years immediately succeeding the Second World War, economic conditions in the Netherlands were poor and prospects seemed low; a public opinion poll in early 1947 showed that about three-fourths of the Dutch adult population felt that they were worse off than they had

been before the war.[3] In these years large-scale emigration
appeared as the only solution to prevent an imminent
overpopulation; this sentiment was expressed in popular
opinion as well as in official government policy.[4] Since
the early fifties, however, the Netherlands has shared in
the spectacular economic expansion enjoyed by all countries in Western Europe. Although in gross domestic
product per capita the Dutch still lag slightly behind most
surrounding nations,[5] the rate of growth has been high.
The past ten years have witnessed a steady increase of
national income; unemployment has been virtually ban-
ished; work conditions have improved, and welfare legislation has brought greater social security; the amount of free
time has increased, and the possibilities of spending it
have grown more varied; mass-produced consumer goods
have become available in better quality and wider range;
and cultural opportunities have generally expanded.[6] As a
result, change has come to be appreciated more and more
as a positive value. The expression "the good old times"
still lingers in Dutch idiom, but it is mostly used in a
derogatory manner, implying that the good old times are a
legend, and that the present is really to be preferred.
When asked, most Dutchmen nowadays declare to be
content with their lot; an extensive satisfaction survey a
few years ago revealed a "strikingly positive picture." [7]

National unity is related to both continuity and change.
Three and a half centuries of national existence have
made Dutch society a close-knit, distinctive whole. The
Dutch social structure is clearly demarcated by the national boundaries; Dutch culture is a unique variant of
the Western European pattern. In this study we have
only in passing touched upon the problem of national
character, but certainly there appear to be some common
Dutch traits noted again and again by foreign observers.[8]
Modernization has intensified national unity by establish-

ing more frequent and regular contacts between various sections of the population, thus enhancing social cohesion and cultural uniformity.

Again, diversity need not be contrary to unity. Any societal whole is composed of diverse parts, differentiated if only by age and sex. Unity need not be impaired by this kind of diversity, nor by differences of residence, creed, and socioeconomic status. In Dutch society most manifestations of public conflict center around the latter two divisions. Being interwoven in the intricate system of *verzuiling,* however, these overt conflicts appear to be furthering rather than lessening national integration in the long run. In the process of "segmented integration" religious differences and economic inequalities have been jointly incorporated in the institutional pattern of Dutch society, safeguarding unity as well as diversity. Indeed, the conscious commitment to the values of both unity and diversity seems to be one of the key aspects of Dutch society; expressed in the idea of tolerance, this twofold commitment has always been a prominent tenet in the national ideology.

The idea of tolerance is matched by the idea of orderliness. Nonconformity in thought and religion is tolerated as long as it does not interfere with the prevailing social order. At points where the norm of orderliness is supposed to be violated, the tolerance of the social system ends, and divergence comes to be defined as "deviance." [9]

We have not been able to deal with the problem of deviance in this brief study. It would seem, however, that in stressing the orderly institutional aspects, we have brought out the more salient and distinctive features of Dutch society. Every society requires a balance between continuity and change, between unity and diversity. In the Netherlands this balance is maintained in a markedly ordered way.

Notes

I. Introduction

1. This becomes 98 per cent when we include people born in the former Dutch colonies in Southeast Asia and South America. See Netherlands Central Bureau of Statistics, *Statistical Year Book of the Netherlands, 1961-1962* (Zeist: W. de Haan, 1964), p. 14.

2. Georg Simmel, *The Sociology of Georg Simmel*, Kurt H. Wolff, trans. (Glencoe, Ill.: Free Press, 1950), p. 10.

II. Historical Perspective

1. Pieter Geyl, *The Revolt of the Netherlands, 1555-1609*, 2nd ed. (New York: Barnes and Noble, 1958); Pieter Geyl, *History of the Low Countries: Episodes and Problems* (New York: Macmillan, 1964), pp. 1-22; G. J. Renier, *The Dutch Nation: An Historical Study* (London: Allen and Unwin, 1944); Bernard M. H. Vlekke, *Evolution of the Dutch Nation* (New York: Roy Publishers, 1945).

2. Renier, *op. cit.*, p. 81. For an analysis of the Dutch revolt in terms of Crane Brinton's model of revolutions, see the contributions by Gordon Griffith, Georg Nadel, and I. Schöf-

fer in *Comparative Studies in Society and History*, II (1960), 452-84; and III (1961), 470-77.

3. John Lothrop Motley, *The Rise of the Dutch Republic*, 3 vols. (New York: Harper and Brothers, 1855).

4. See Seymour Martin Lipset, *The First New Nation: The United States in Historical and Comparative Perspective* (New York: Basic Books, 1963), pp. 13-98. A further comparison of the early development of the two Republics along the lines suggested by Lipset would probably lead to some interesting analogies.

5. Lipset, *op. cit.*, p. 45.

6. An extensive bibliography on Dutch colonial history may be found in W. Ph. Coolhaas, *A Critical Survey of Studies on Dutch Colonial History* ('s Gravenhage: Martinus Nijhoff, 1960). To this may be added some more recent works, such as C. R. Boxer, *The Dutch Seaborne Empire, 1600-1800* (New York: Knopf, 1965); D. W. Davies, *A Primer of Dutch Seventeenth Century Overseas Trade* (The Hague: Martinus Nijhoff, 1961); George Masselman, *The Cradle of Colonialism* (New Haven: Yale University Press, 1963). All of these works deal with the early Dutch colonists abroad; there is no monograph probing the impact of the colonial experience upon the mother country. For a comparative study of Dutch and British colonialism in Asia in the twentieth century, see J. S. Furnivall, *Colonial Policy and Practice: A Comparative Study of Burma and Netherlands India* (London: Cambridge University Press, 1948). The breakup of the colonial empire in Asia is described in Leslie H. Palmier, *Indonesia and the Dutch* (London: Oxford University Press, 1962).

7. "It is beyond doubt that the economic growth of the Dutch Republic during its Golden Age was largely due to forces other than the Protestant ethic as defined by Max Weber." W. F. Wertheim, *East-West Parallels* (The Hague: W. van Hoeve, 1964), p. 150. For a thorough critique of the Weber-Troeltsch thesis, see also Albert Hyma, "Calvinism and Capitalism in the Netherlands, 1555-1700," *Journal of Modern History*, X (1938), 321-43.

8. Renier, *op. cit.*, p. 23.

9. I. J. Brugmans, *Paardenkracht en mensenmacht: Sociaaleconomische geschiedenis van Nederland 1795-1940* (The Hague: Martinus Nijhoff, 1960), p. 102.

10. J. Pen and P. J. Bouman, "Een eeuw van toenemende welvaart," in A. N. J. den Hollander et al. (eds.), *Drift en koers: Een halve eeuw sociale verandering in Nederland*, (Assen: Van Gorcum & Co., 1961); pp. 85-104.

11. Aris van Braam, *Ambtenaren en bureaucratie in Nederland* ('s Gravenhage: Excelsior Foto-Offset, 1957), pp. 34-36.

12. See Gerald L. Burke, *The Making of Dutch Towns* (London: Cleaver-Hume Press, 1956), pp. 141-53; Lewis Mumford, *The City in History* (London: Secker & Warburg, 1961), pp. 439-45.

13. David Riesman, *The Lonely Crowd: A Study of the Changing American Character*, new ed. (New Haven: Yale University Press, 1961), p. xxix.

14. It will be understood that "national" is here contrasted with "local," and not with "international." A great deal of Dutch national culture plainly derives from international sources.

15. J. H. A. Elemans, *Woord en wereld van de boer* (Utrecht: Het Spectrum, 1958), p. 9.

16. On Friesland, see the special Friesland issue of *Delta*, VIII (Winter 1965-1966).

17. See Chapter III.

18. See J. Goudsblom, "Het algemeen beschaafd Nederlands," *Sociologische Gids*, XI (1964), 106-24.

19. On "civility," see Norbert Elias, *Über den Prozess der Zivilisation*, 2 vols. (Basel: Haus zum Falken, 1939). For a shorter statement in English, see Norbert Elias and John L. Scotson, *The Established and the Outsiders* (London: Frank Cass & Co., 1965), pp. 152-53. The term "civility" is used here in a quite different sense than by Edward A. Shils in "Ideology and Civility," *Sewanee Review*, LXVI (1958), 450-80; and in other papers.

20. For a discussion by an American sociologist, see David O. Moberg, "Social Differentiation in the Netherlands," *Social Forces*, XXXIX (1960-61), 333-37.

21. A. Chorus, *De Nederlander uiterlijk en innerlijk* (Leiden: A. W. Sijthoff, 1964), p. 119.

22. See G. J. Kruijer, *Hongertochten* (Meppel: J. A. Boom, 1951), on the social disorganization of Amsterdam in the winter 1944-1945. Another catastrophic episode was the flood that ravaged great parts of Zeeland and southern South

Holland in February, 1953. See J. E. Ellemers, *De Februari-ramp: Sociologie van een samenleving in nood* (Assen: Van Gorcum & Co., 1956), and the joint report of the Instituut voor Sociaal Onderzoek van het Nederlandse Volk (Isonevo) and the Committee on Disaster Studies of the National Academy of Sciences, *Studies in Holland Flood Disaster 1953*, 4 vols. (Washington, D.C.: National Research Council, 1955). See also Ch. VI, note 1.

III. Demographic Composition and Social Differentiation

1. E. W. Hofstee, *Rural Life and Rural Welfare in the Netherlands* (The Hague: Government Printing and Publishing Office, 1957), p. 178.

2. William Petersen, *Planned Migration: The Social Determinants of the Dutch-Canadian Movement* (Berkeley: University of California Press, 1955), p. 15.

3. F. van Heek, *Het geboorte-niveau der Nederlandse Rooms-Katholieken* (Leiden: H. E. Stenfert Kroese, 1954); E. W. Hofstee, "Regionale verscheidenheid in de ontwikkeling van het aantal geboorten in Nederland in de tweede helft van de 19 eeuw," in *Akademiedagen*, VII (1954), 59-106; E. W. Hofstee, "De groei van de Nederlandse bevolking," in A. N. J. den Hollander et al. (eds.), *Drift en koers: Een halve eeuw sociale verandering in Nederland* (Assen: Van Gorcum & Co., 1961), pp. 13-84; F. van Heek, "Het Nederlandse geboortepatroon en de godsdienstfactor gedurende de laatste halve eeuw," *Mens en Maatschappij*, XXXVIII (1963), 81-103, 257-68; E. W. Hofstee, "Het proces der geboortedaling in Nederland 1850-1960," *Mens en Maatschappij*, XXXVIII (1963), 104-33, 269-77. For an English summary of Van Heek's original study, see F. van Heek, "Roman Catholicism and Fertility in the Netherlands: Demographic Aspects of Minority Status," *Population Studies*, X (1956), 125-38. For a commentary on the Van Heek-Hofstee discussion, see William Petersen, "Fertility Trends and Population Policy," *Sociologia Neerlandica*, III (1966).

4. William Petersen, "The Demographic Transition in the Netherlands," *American Sociological Review*, XXV (1960), 334-47.

5. See also William Petersen, "Family Subsidies in the

Netherlands," *Marriage and Family Living,* XVII (1955), 260-66.

6. For the concept of synchronization, see Wilbert E. Moore, *Man, Time, and Society* (New York: Wiley and Sons, 1963).

7. J. A. Ponsioen, "De jeugd als nieuwe leeftijdsgroep in ontwikkelingslanden," *Mens en Maatschappij,* XXXVIII (1963), 134-45.

8. Robert K. Merton, *Social Theory and Social Structure,* rev. ed. (New York: The Free Press, 1957), pp. 131-94.

9. In 1957 the average age of mayors of towns of over 20,000 inhabitants was 55; none was under 40. A. van Braam, "Aspecten van de selectie en sociale mobiliteit der Nederlandse burgemeesters van grote gemeenten," *Mens en Maatschappij,* XXXIV (1959), 43-52. In 1960, of all millionaires, 83 per cent were over 50. Centraal Bureau voor de Statistiek, *Inkomstenverdeling 1959 en vermogensverdeling 1960* (Zeist: W. de Haan, 1963), p. 28.

10. See David Riesman, *Faces in the Crowd: Individual Studies in Character and Politics* (New Haven: Yale University Press, 1951), pp. 7-9.

11. For some interesting attempts, see A. H. M. Romein-Verschoor, "Jeugd en ouderdom," *Sociologisch Jaarboek,* VIII (1954), 65-94; G. J. Harmsen, *Blauwe en rode jeugd* (Assen: Van Gorcum & Co., 1961); J. S. van Hessen, *Samen jong zijn* (Assen: Van Gorcum & Co., 1965).

12. P. Vinke, *De maatschappelijke plaats en herkomst der directeuren en commissarissen van de open en daarmede vergelijkbare besloten naamloze vennootschappen* (Leiden: H. E. Stenfert Kroese, 1961), p. 140.

13. See M. Staverman, *Buitenkerkelijkheid in Friesland* (Assen: Van Gorcum & Co., 1954), pp. 41-46.

14. C. N. Impeta, *Kaart van kerkelijk Nederland,* 2nd ed. (Kampen: J. H. Kok, 1964), p. 98.

15. M. A. J. M. Matthijsen, *Katholiek middelbaar onderwijs en intellectuele emancipatie* (Assen: Van Gorcum & Co., 1958), pp. 127-29; F. Verhage, "Intelligentie en kerkelijke gezindte," *Nederlands Tijdschrift voor de Psychologie,* XIX (1964), 247-54.

16. I. Gadourek, *A Dutch Community,* 2nd ed. (Groningen: J. B. Wolters, 1961), pp. 112-13. For similar findings, see A. K. Constandse, "Acquaintanceships of Farmers in a

Newly Colonized Area," *Sociaal Kompas,* VI (1958-1959), 69-74; and G. Kuiper, *Mobiliteit in de sociale en beroeps-hiërarchie* (Assen: Van Gorcum & Co., 1954).

17. B. van Leeuwen, *Het gemengde huwelijk* (Assen: Van Gorcum & Co., 1959).

18. Gadourek, *op. cit.,* pp. 97-100.

19. P. Kloos, "Traditionele onkerksheid in Drente," *Mens en Maatschappij,* XXXVI (1961), 423-30; J. de Leeuwe, "Ontwikkeling in de richting van ongodsdienstigheid," *Mens en Maatschappij,* XXXIX (1964), 9-28.

20. Rijksdienst voor het Nationale Plan, and Centraal Planbureau, *Het Westen en overig Nederland* ('s Gravenhage: Staatsdrukkerij, 1956); J. Winsemius, "Urbanization in the Western Part of the Netherlands (Randstad Holland)," *Tijdschrift voor Economische en Sociale Geografie,* LI (1960), 188-99.

21. I. Gadourek, *Riskante gewoonten en zorg voor eigen welzijn* (Groningen: J. B. Wolters, 1963), p. 312.

22. A. K. Constandse, *Boer en toekomstbeeld* (Wageningen: Afdeling Sociologie en Sociografie van de Landbouwhogeschool, 1964).

23. See *Lezerskringonderzoek Margriet,* 4 vols. (Amsterdam: Geillustreerde Pers, 1962).

24. W. Steigenga, *Moderne planologie* (Utrecht: Aula Boeken, 1964), p. 84.

25. M. van de Vall, *De vakbeweging in de welvaartsstaat* (Meppel: J. A. Boom & Zoon, 1963), p. 22; Seymour M. Lipset and Reinhard Bendix, *Social Mobility in Industrial Society* (Berkeley: University of California Press, 1959), pp. 273-74.

26. Centraal Bureau voor de Statistiek, *Vrije-tijdsbesteding in Nederland: Winter 1955/56,* vol. 8 (Zeist: W. de Haan, 1959), p. 34.

27. J. A. A. van Doorn, *Sociale ongelijkheid en sociaal beleid* (Utrecht: Bijleveld, 1963), p. 12.

28. *Ibid.,* p. 127.

29. For detailed data on mobility to the chief executive ranks, see Vinke, *op. cit.,* pp. 129-202. See also R. A. Hendriks, "The Vertical Mobility of the Chief Executive Groups in the Netherlands," *Sociologia Neerlandica,* II (Summer 1964), 63-76.

30. *Vrije-tijdsbesteding in Nederland, op. cit.,* p. 31.

31. Reports in English on these and related studies by Jacques A. A. van Doorn, F. van Heek, E. W. Hofstee, Ida van Hulten, P. J. Idenburg, G. Kuiper, A. W. Luijckx, J. J. M. van Tulder, and P. Vinke may be found in *Transactions of the Third World Congress of Sociology*, vols. II, III, and VII (London: International Sociological Association, 1954-1957). For the present discussion I have drawn heavily upon J. J. M. van Tulder, *De Beroepsmobiliteit in Nederland van 1919 tot 1954* (Leiden: H. E. Stenfert Kroese, 1962).

32. See S. M. Miller, "Comparative Social Mobility," *Current Sociology*, IX (1960), 1-89.

33. An exception should be made for the excellent study of P. Vinke, *op. cit.* (see above, notes 12 and 29).

IV. National Integration

1. See Reinhard Bendix on "the modern duality between government and society: a nationwide jurisdiction with administrative authority in the hands of a functionally defined group of officials on the one hand, and formally equal participation in public affairs by all citizens on the other," in *Nation-Building and Citizenship* (New York: John Wiley and Sons, 1964), p. 128.

2. See Aris van Braam, *Ambtenaren en bureaucratie in Nederland* ('s Gravenhage: Excelsior Foto-Offset, 1957), pp. 20-63.

3. For one study, see C. J. Lammers, "Midshipmen and Candidate Reserve Officers at the Royal Netherlands Naval College: A Comparative Study of a Socialization Process," *Sociologia Neerlandica*, II, 2 (Summer 1965), 98-123.

4. See Amry Vandenbosch, *Dutch Foreign Policy Since 1815: A Study in Small Power Politics* (The Hague: Martinus Nijhoff, 1959).

5. For the distinction between civil, political, and social rights, see T. H. Marshall: *Class, Citizenship, and Social Development* (Garden City, N.Y.: Anchor Books, 1965), pp. 78-79.

6. Gunnar Myrdal, *Beyond the Welfare State* (New Haven: Yale University Press, 1960), p. 61.

7. For a comprehensive survey of postwar economic policy in the Netherlands, see J. E. Andriesen, "Economic Developments in the Netherlands," *Planning and Development in*

the Netherlands, I, 1 (Spring 1962), 29-36; John Z. F. Lewandowski, "Recent Trends in the Dutch Economy," *The World Today,* XX (1964), 403-10.

8. On the authorities and functions of these organizations, see Ellen M. Bussey, "Recent Wage Control Policy in the Netherlands," *Monthly Labor Review,* LXXXVII (1964), 517-21; see also J. Pen, "The Strange Adventures of Dutch Wage Policy," *British Journal of Industrial Relations,* I (1963), 318-30; and B. C. Roberts, *National Wages Policy in War and Peace* (London: Allen and Unwin, 1958), pp. 118-34.

9. Myrdal, *op. cit.,* pp. 117-30.

10. For this section I have drawn heavily upon the papers by Hans Daalder, "Parties and Politics in the Netherlands," *Political Studies,* III (1955), 1-16; "The Relationship Between Cabinet and Parliament in the Netherlands," International Political Science Association, Rome Congress, 1958 (mimeographed); and "The Netherlands: Opposition in a Segmented Society," in Robert A. Dahl, ed., *Political Oppositions in Western Democracies* (New Haven: Yale University Press, 1966), pp. 188-236. The reader is also referred to Robert C. Bone, "The Dynamics of Dutch Politics," *Journal of Politics,* XXIV (1962), 23-49, and A. Hoogerwerf, "Latent Socio-Political Issues in the Netherlands," *Sociologica Neerlandica,* II (1965), 161-79.

11. Centraal Bureau voor de Statistiek, *Statistiek der Verkiezingen* (Zeist: W. de Haan, 1963), p. 8.

12. On the extreme left, see Frits Kool, "Communism in Holland: A Study in Futility," *Problems of Communism,* IX, 5 (Sept.-Oct. 1960), 17-24.

13. Daalder, "Parties and Politics," pp. 6-7.

14. J. K. Galbraith, *Economics and the Art of Controversy* (New York: Vintage Books, 1959), p. 77.

15. For an extensive English summary, see Lucas van der Land, Constance E. van der Maesen, and Peter R. Baehr, "Voting in the Netherlands: A Panel Study in an Amsterdam Suburb," International Political Science Association, Sixth World Congress, Geneva, 1964 (mimeographed).

16. For slightly diverging national figures, see J. J. de Jong, *Overheid en onderdaan* (Wageningen: Zomer en Keuning, 1956), p. 103.

17. Centraal Bureau voor de Statistiek, *Dertiende Al-*

gemene Volkstelling 31 mei 1960, vol. VIII B (Zeist: W. de Haan, 1964), p. 15.

18. J. J. M. van Tulder: *De beroepsmobiliteit in Nederland van 1919 tot 1954* (Leiden: H. H. Stenfert Kroese, 1962), p. 119.

19. P. J. Idenburg, *Schets van het Nederlandse schoolwezen,* 2nd ed. (Groningen: J. B. Wolters, 1964), p. 166; Centraal Bureau voor de Statistiek, *Dertiende Algemene Volkstelling 31 mei 1960,* vol. IX (Zeist: W. de Haan, 1964), p. 14.

20. For detailed figures on differential university enrollment, see Centraal Bureau voor de Statistiek, *De sociale en regionale herkomst der studenten bij het Hoger Onderwijs 1958-1959* (Zeist: W. de Haan, 1960).

21. F. van Heek, "Sociale ongelijkwaardigheid en verticale mobiliteit in de 20e eeuw: wijzigingen en continuïteit," in A. N. J. den Hollander et al. (eds.), *Drift en koers: Een halve eeuw sociale verandering in Nederland* (Assen: Van Gorcum & Co., 1961), pp. 149-179, especially pp. 169ff.

22. See A. H. Halsey (ed.), *Ability and Educational Opportunity* (Paris: Organisation for Economic Cooperation and Development, 1961), p. 32.

23. See Basil Bernstein, "Social Class and Linguistic Development: A Theory of Social Learning," in A. H. Halsey, Jean Floud, and C. Arnold Anderson (eds.), *Education, Economy, and Society* (New York: The Free Press, 1961), pp. 288-314.

24. As M. van de Poel demonstrates, scholastic failure in secondary school is far more likely to cause dropouts among students from working class than from middle or upper class families. See M. van de Poel, "Milieu van herkomst en schoolsucces," *Onderwijs en Opvoeding,* XV (1964), 144-49.

25. Marshall, *op. cit.,* p. 119.

26. For quantitative evidence, see Van Tulder, *op. cit.,* pp. 119-26.

27. See I. Gadourek, *A Dutch Community,* 2nd ed. (Groningen: J. B. Wolters, 1961), pp. 200-07.

28. J. P. Kruijt, *Verzuiling* (Zaandijk: Heijnis, 1959), pp. 24-27.

29. For these and comparative figures, see Bureau of Statistics of the European Communities, *Basic Statistics of the Community 1964* (Brussels, 1964), p. 101.

30. Theodor Geiger, *Die Klassengesellschaft im Schmelz-tiegel* (Köln: Gustav Kiepenheuer, 1949), pp. 182-95. See also Arthur M. Ross and Paul T. Hartmann, *Changing Patterns of Industrial Conflict* (New York: Wiley, 1960).

31. See Fr. de Jong Edz., *Om de plaats van de arbeid* (Amsterdam: Arbeiderspers, 1956).

32. See E. Abma, *Leiding en leden in landbouwcoöperaties* (Meppel: J. A. Boom, 1962); P. J. A. ter Hoeven, *Havenarbeiders van Amsterdam en Rotterdam* (Leiden: H. E. Stenfert Kroese, 1963); M. van de Vall, *De vakbeweging in de welvaartstaat* (Meppel: J. A. Boom, 1963). See also for further reference Jan Berting, "Industrial Sociology in the Netherlands Since the Second World War," *Sociologia Neerlandica* III (1965-66), 2-27.

33. J. E. Andriessen, S. Miedema, and C. J. Oort, *De sociaal-economische besturing van Nederland* (Groningen: P. Noordhof, no date), pp. 54, 68, 72.

34. *Ibid.,* p. 72. See also Alan D. Robinson, *Dutch Organized Agriculture in International Politics, 1945-1960* (The Hague: Martinus Nijhoff, 1961).

35. Myrdal, *op. cit.,* p. 134.

36. Maarten Schneider, *De Nederlandse krant,* 2nd ed. (Amsterdam: P. N. van Kampen en Zoon, 1949), p. 151.

37. Centraal Bureau voor de Statistiek, *Vrije-tijdsbesteding in Nederland: Winter 1955/56,* vol. V (Zeist: W. de Haan, 1957), p. 10.

38. Centraal Bureau voor de Statistiek, *Statistiek van de vrije jeugdvorming 1963* (Zeist: W. de Haan, 1964), p. 11.

39. C. Miermans, *Voetbal in Nederland* (Assen: Van Gorcum & Co., 1955); M. Rooij (ed.), *Voetballen toen en nu* (Utrecht: Koninklijke Nederlandse Voetbalbond, 1964).

40. Centraal Bureau voor de Statistiek, *Vrije-tijdsbesteding in Nederland 1962-1963,* vol. I (Zeist: W. de Haan, 1964), p. 45.

41. *Ibid.,* pp. 22-24.

42. Centraal Bureau voor de Statistiek, *Vrije-tijdsbesteding in Nederland 1962-1963,* vol. IV (Zeist: W. de Haan, 1965).

43. These and the following data on Dutch newspapers are derived from mimeographed communications, dated March 31, 1965, from Cebuco, the Central Bureau for Newspaper Publicity in Amsterdam.

44. H. Hoefnagels, *Een eeuw sociale problematiek* (Assen: Van Gorcum & Co., 1956), p. 61.

45. See J. D. Dengerink, *Critisch-historisch onderzoek naar de sociologische ontwikkeling van het beginsel der "Souvereiniteit in eigen kring" in de 19e en 20e eeuw* (Kampen: J. H. Kok, 1948).

46. See the theoretical observations by Lewis A. Coser, *The Functions of Social Conflict* (Glencoe, Ill.: Free Press, 1956), esp. pp. 72-85.

47. For a critical analysis of the priority given to "social peace" and orderliness, see H. Hoefnagels, "Nederland een sociaal paradijs?" *Sociologische Gids*, VIII (1961), 274-89.

48. For a balanced account of "pillarizing" and "depillarizing" tendencies, see J. P. Kruijt and Walter Goddijn, "Verzuiling en ontzuiling als sociologisch proces," in A. N. J. den Hollander et al. (eds.), *Drift en koers: Een halve eeuw sociale verandering in Nederland* (Assen: Van Gorcum & Co. 1961), pp. 227-63, esp. pp. 245-49.

49. For the degree of *zuil* identification in various sections of the population, see I. Gadourek, J. Oorburg, and L. T. van de Laar, "Involvement in Cultural System in the Netherlands: Its Measurement and Social Correlates," *Social Forces*, XL (1961-1962), 302-08. See also J. Weima, "Authoritarianism, Religious Conservatism, and Sociocentric Attitudes in Roman Catholic Groups," *Human Relations*, XVIII (1965), 231-39.

50. J. de Kadt, *Ketterse kanttekeningen* (Amsterdam: G. A. van Oorschot, 1965), pp. 157-63.

51. Thus David O. Moberg has propounded the thesis that "the Dutch pattern of vertical pluralism (the *verzuiling*) could become the future American pattern of religion-society relationships," in "Religion and Society in the Netherlands and in America," *American Quarterly*, XIII (1961), 172-78. See also Gerhard E. Lenski, *The Religious Factor*, rev. ed. (Garden City, N.Y.: Anchor Books, 1963), pp. 365-66.

V. Family and Community

1. For an account of Dutch kinship, see H. T. Fischer, "Het Nederlandse verwantschapsysteem," *Mens en Maatschappij*, XXII (1947), 104-17.

2. For rural family styles, see C. D. Saal, *Het boerengezin in Nederland* (Assen: Van Gorcum & Co., 1958); E. W.

Hofstee, *Rural Life and Rural Welfare in the Netherlands* (The Hague: Government Printing and Publishing Office, 1957), pp. 321-30.

3. K. Ishwaran, *Family Life in the Netherlands* (The Hague: Van Keulen N. V., 1959); M. M. Peters-Nanninga, "Family Life in the Netherlands," *Mens en Maatschappij*, XXXVII (1962), 352-59.

4. See Jan Pen, "The Priority of Housing," *Delta*, VI, 2 (Summer 1963), 17-31.

5. See I. Gadourek, *A Dutch Community*, 2nd ed. (Groningen: J. B. Wolters, 1961), pp. 107-09.

6. The figures on family size, marital state, divorce, and suicide are based upon two publications of the Netherlands Central Bureau of Statistics, *Zestig jaren statistiek in tijdreeksen 1899-1959* (Zeist: W. de Haan, 1959), pp. 10-18; and *Statistisch Zakboek 1965* (Hilversum: W. de Haan, 1965), pp. 5-12, 179.

7. H. Philipsen, "Gezin en vrijetijdsbesteding in het sociaalwetenschappelijk onderzoek," *Sociologische Gids*, X (1963), 306-21.

8. Rijksdienst voor het Nationale Plan, *Mensen op Zondag* (The Hague: Staatsdrukkerij, 1962), pp. 125-40.

9. G. A. Kooij, *Het veranderend gezin in Nederland* (Leerdam: Ter Haar en Schuijt, 1957), p. 164.

10. W. H. Douma, *Het gezin op een verstedelijkend platteland* (Wageningen: Afdeling Sociologie en Sociografie van de Landbouwhogeschool, 1961).

11. United Nations, *Statistical Yearbook 1964* (New York, 1965), p. 712.

12. Louis Couperus, *Old People and the Things That Pass,* translated by Alexander Teixeira de Mattos (London: Heinemann, 1963). Better still are the four volumes of the cycle *The Books of the Small Souls,* also translated by Teixeira de Mattos and published in New York by Dodd, Mead and Co.: *Small Souls* (1914), *The Later Life* (1915), *The Twilight of the Souls* (1917), and *Dr. Adriaan* (1918). Unfortunately these translations have been out of print for many years.

13. Robert L. Morlan, "Cabinet Government at the Municipal Level: The Dutch Experience," *The Western Political Quarterly*, XVII (1964), 317-24.

14. H. A. M. C. Dibbits, *Nederland waterland: een*

historisch-technisch overzicht (Utrecht: A. Oosthoek, 1950), pp. 88-91, 152-76. See also Johan van Veen, *Dredge, Drain, Reclaim: The Art of a Nation,* 5th ed. (The Hague: Martinus Nijhoff, 1962).

15. A. K. Constandse, *Het dorp in de IJsselmeerpolders* (Zwolle: W. E. J. Tjeenk Willink, 1960), pp. 165-66.

16. A. J. Wichers: *Leven en werken te Elim-Hollandsche-veld* (Assen: Van Gorcum & Co., 1959), pp. 51-52.

17. Ernst Abma, "Participation in Community Services: A Case Study of the Health Service," *Sociologia Ruralis,* I (1960), 43-50, at 49.

18. John Y. Keur and Dorothy L. Keur, *The Deeply Rooted: A Study of a Drents Community in the Netherlands* (Assen: Van Gorcum & Co., 1955), pp. 90-91.

19. *Ibid.,* p. 103.

20. See G. Beijer, *Rural Migrants in an Urban Setting* (The Hague: Martinus Nijhoff, 1963), pp. 170-204.

21. Michael Young and Peter Willmott, *Family and Kinship in East London* (London: Routledge & Kegan Paul, 1957); F. Grünfeld and J. Weima, *Leven in een Rotterdamse randzone* (Rotterdam: Gemeentelijke Dienst voor Sociale Zaken, 1957); J. Simonse, "Sociologische schets van de volksbuurt," *De Schalm,* XX (1963), pp. 1-127.

22. W. Steigenga, *Moderne planologie* (Utrecht: Aula Boeken, 1964), pp. 114-16.

23. F. Grünfeld, *Veenzicht: Leven in een na-oorlogse woonwijk* (Rotterdam: Gemeentelijke Dienst voor Sociale Zaken, 1959). For an English summary, see *Sociologia Neerlandica,* I (1963), 71-74.

VI. Conclusion

1. See Werner Warmbrunn, *The Dutch Under the German Occupation 1940-1945* (Stanford, Calif.: Stanford University Press, 1963).

2. See B. Benvenuti, *Farming in Cultural Change* (Assen: Van Gorcum & Co., 1962); F. Bergsma, *Op weg naar een nieuw cultuurpatroon* (Assen: Van Gorcum & Co., 1963); A. W. van den Ban, *Boer en landbouwvoorlichting* (Assen: Van Gorcum & Co., 1963).

3. Quoted by B. P. Hofstede: *Thwarted Exodus: Post-War Overseas Migration from the Netherlands* (The Hague: Martinus Nijhoff, 1964), p. 21.

4. See Hofstede, *op. cit.* See also G. Beijer (ed.), *Characteristics of Overseas Emigrants* (The Hague: Government Publishing Office, 1961); William Petersen, *Planned Migration: The Social Determinants of the Dutch-Canadian Movement* (Berkeley, Calif.: University of California Press, 1955); J. E. Ellemers, "The Determinants of Emigration: An Analysis of Dutch Studies on Migration," *Sociologia Neerlandica*, II (1964), 41-58.

5. United Nations, Department of Economic and Social Affairs, *Yearbook of National Account Statistics 1964* (New York: United Nations, 1965), pp. 383-92.

6. J. Pen and P. J. Bouman: "Een eeuw van toenemende welvaart," in A. N. J. den Hollander et al. (eds.), *Drift en koers: Een halve eeuw sociale verandering in Nederland* (Assen: Van Gorcum & Co., 1961), pp. 85-104.

7. I. Gadourek, *Riskante gewoonten en zorg voor eigen welzijn* (Groningen: J. B. Wolters, 1963), p. 193. A more substantive corroboration of this verbal response is suggested by the comparatively low incidence of alcoholism and suicide. See Ivan Gadourek, "Drinking and Smoking Habits and the Feeling of Well-being," *Sociologia Neerlandica*, III (1965-66), 28-43; and Cornelis S. Kruijt, "Suicide: A Sociological and Statistical Investigation," *Sociologia Neerlandica*, III (1965-66), 44-59. See also I. Gadourek, *Absences and Well-being of Workers* (Groningen: J. B. Wolters, 1965). For literature on mental health, see the bibliography by E. Tellegen, "Sociale problematiek in de psychiatrie en geestelijke gezondheidszorg," *Mens en Maatschappij*, XLI (1966), 117-34.

8. H. C. J. Duijker and N. H. Frijda, *National Character and National Stereotypes* (Amsterdam: North Holland Publishing Company, 1960), p. 109. See also G. Brugmans, *Onder de loupe van het buitenland* (Baarn: Hollandse Drukkerij, 1929); A. N. J. den Hollander, "Heeft Nederland een eigen volkskarakter?", *De Kern*, XXXV, 9 (Sept. 1965), 6-12.

9. There is an extensive literature in Dutch on the theoretical implications of the concept of deviance or *onmaatschappelijkheid* ("unsociability"). For a cogent analysis, see P. Milikowski, *Sociale aanpassing, niet-aanpassing, onmaatschappelijkheid* (Arnhem: Van Loghum Slaterus, 1961). See also R. R. Koopmans, "Vijf studies over onmaatschappelijkheid," *Sociologische Gids*, IX (1962), 329-35.

Bibliographical Note

There is no comprehensive study of Dutch society comparable to, for example, *American Society* by Robin M. Williams, Jr. The main special studies are mentioned in the footnotes to each chapter of the present book; we have tried to include all important publications in English.

The two books that come closest to a comprehensive survey of Dutch society are readers, one in Dutch—A. N. J. den Hollander et al. (eds.), *Drift en koers: Een halve eeuw sociale verandering in Nederland* (Assen: Van Gorcum & Co., 1961), and one in German—Joachim Matthes (ed.), *Soziologie und Gesellschaft in den Niederlanden* (Neuwied: Hermann Luchterhand, 1965).

Since 1963 there is an English-language periodical, *Sociologia Neerlandica,* intended to reflect the development of Dutch sociology. Studies in English on particular aspects of Dutch society may also be found from time to time in *Sociologia Ruralis,* concerned with rural sociology, and in *Social Compass,* concerned with the sociology of religion. The quarterly *Delta* offers information on "arts, life, and thought in the Netherlands," including a checklist of recent English-language books about the Netherlands.

The main sociological journals in Dutch are *Mens en Maatschappij* (since 1925), *Sociologische Gids* (since 1954), and *Sociale Wetenschappen* (since 1957).

Systematic bibliographies of Dutch sociology are contained in J. A. A. van Doorn, "The Development of Sociology and Social Research in the Netherlands," *Mens en Maatschappij*, XXXI (1956), 189-264; and in J. A. A. van Doorn, *Beeld en betekenis van de Nederlandse sociologie* (Utrecht: Bijleveld, 1964), pp. 167-215. For general bibliographical information, see A. M. P. Mollema: *Bibliographia Neerlandica I: Books on the Netherlands in Foreign Languages, 1940-1957* (The Hague: Martinus Nijhoff, 1962).

Detailed statistical information on many aspects of Dutch society may be found in the publications of the Netherlands Central Bureau of Statistics, The Hague. All publications contain English explanations and summaries.

Index

STUDIES IN SOCIOLOGY